ASHCROFT

ASHCROFT

Robert Tanitch

HUTCHINSON
LONDON MELBOURNE AUCKLAND JOHANNESBURG

For Shirley Levy

Also by Robert Tanitch

A Pictorial Companion to Shakespeare's Plays
Ralph Richardson, A Tribute
Olivier
Leonard Rossiter

Frontispiece: Cleopatra in *Antony and Cleopatra*   1950

© Robert Tanitch 1987

This edition first published in 1987 by Hutchinson, an imprint of
Century Hutchinson Ltd, Brookmount House, 62-65 Chandos Place, London WC2N 4NW

Century Hutchinson Australia Pty Ltd
PO Box 496, 16-22 Church Street, Hawthorn, Victoria 3122, Australia

Century Hutchinson New Zealand Limited
PO Box 40-086, Glenfield, Auckland 10, New Zealand

Century Hutchinson South Africa (Pty) Ltd
PO Box 337, Berglvei, 2012 South Africa

Printed and Bound in Great Britain by
Butler & Tanner Ltd, Frome, Somerset

CONTENTS

WITH TRIBUTES BY

Edward Albee   Harry Andrews   Judi Dench
Gwen Ffrangcon-Davies   Peter Hall   John Gielgud   Alec Guinness
Christopher Morahan   Motley   Trevor Nunn
Laurence Olivier   Harold Pinter   Anthony Quayle   Dorothy Tutin

INTRODUCTION

PEGGY ASHCROFT is acknowledged by the acting profession, by the public and critics alike, to be one of the great actresses of the twentieth century. This book, which celebrates her eightieth birthday, is a pictorial record and full chronology of her career in theatre, film and television, from the 1920s to the present day.

When asked, in those very rare interviews she has given so reluctantly over the years, who has been the greatest influence in her life, she almost invariably has answered that Shakespeare has. Her love for him, which began with reading the plays and reading about Henry Irving and Ellen Terry at the Lyceum Theatre in the last century, was continued at school, where she was encouraged to act him as well.

Her career has been notable for its commitment to theatre, and to classical and modern classical theatre in particular. She has played twenty roles by Shakespeare, five by Ibsen, and four by Chekhov. She has acted in Greek tragedy, Jacobean drama, eighteenth-century comedy and the theatre of the absurd. She has been in plays by Shaw, Bulgakov, Wilde, Brecht and Grass. She has appeared in two plays by Marguerite Duras, two by Edward Albee and two by Harold Pinter.

She has been involved in most of the major pioneering theatrical movements of the last six decades. She was a member of John Gielgud's companies in his New, Queen's and Haymarket Theatre seasons in the 1930s and 1940s. In the 1950s and 1960s she was in at the inception of both the English Stage Company and the Royal Shakespeare Company. In the 1970s she acted at the National Theatre.

She has worked with the leading directors of the day, including John Gielgud, Theodore Komisarjevsky, Michel Saint-Denis, Glen Byam Shaw, George Devine, Peter Hall and Trevor Nunn.

She has played an extraordinary range of parts: everything from romantic *ingenues* and crazy old women to queens and prostitutes. She has been cast as a temple dancing-girl, a three-hundred-year-old ghost, a dypsomaniac, a gigolo's mother, a schizophrenic, an ex-circus performer, a curator of an art museum ('Call me Lady Gee, everybody does'), a retired missionary schoolteacher and a seaside landlady.

She has played a Belgian nun, a Norwegian rat-catcher, three formidable American matriarchs and a Chinese business*man*.

She has created roles for Somerset Maugham, John Drinkwater, Beverley Nichols, Rodney Ackland, Clemence Dane, Robert Morley and Noel Langley, Terence Rattigan, William Douglas Home, Ruth Prawer Jhabvala, Stephen Poliakoff and Dennis Potter.

On stage she has murdered and been murdered. She has gone to prison and been reprieved. She has committed suicide on any number of occasions, jumping out of windows backwards and generally drowning, poisoning and shooting herself. She has also tried to gas herself and failed.

She has appeared in two Ministry of Information films, a Marxist parable and a piece of anti-Fascist propaganda. She has had one of her performances stopped by anti-Nazi demonstrators. She has acted a number of real people, including the wives of two Russian authors, the widow of a murdered communist leader, a famous actress having a platonic affair with a famous critic, and a theatre manager haranguing her audience. She has also played a member of the Royal family in mid-crisis ('Here's a pretty kettle of fish') and a writer of detective fiction who attempts to kill the detective she has created.

On stage or screen, she has been to India three times (and lost her faith twice), travelled second class on the Viennese express and been up the Nile, Congo and Hudson rivers. She has taken her boat to Dunkirk. She has charlestoned in Riga.

She has been wooed by *two* Romeos on alternate nights, giving the line, 'Romeo, Romeo, wherefore art thou Romeo?' an unexpected sub-text. She has spent an illicit weekend in Eastbourne, been jilted in New York, and had a disastrous honeymoon in Cyprus. She has been buried up to her chin in earth and still continued to count her blessings. She has hugged a filthy tramp, taken off all her clothes in a hotel foyer and walked on to the stage carrying her lover's head . . .

Edith Margaret Emily Ashcroft was born at Croydon in Surrey on 22 December 1907. Her father was an estate agent, who was killed during the First World War, and her mother was a keen amateur actress. She was educated at Woodford School, where she acted Shakespeare for the first time, often playing the male leads.

When she was sixteen her mother (who did not live long enough to see her daughter go on the stage) allowed her to attend the Central School of Speech Training and Dramatic Art, though only on the strict understanding that she would not take up acting as a career. There she studied under Elsie Fogerty, the school's founder and principal; in her diploma examination the actress Athene Seyler bracketed her and fellow-student Laurence Olivier with top marks for their performances in the trial scene from *The Merchant of Venice*.

At eighteen, while still at Central, she made her professional debut, with the Birmingham Repertory Company in James Barrie's *Dear Brutus*, taking over the role of the dream-child from an actress who had fallen ill. Her stage father was Ralph Richardson. The following year she was invited back to play the innkeeper's daughter in John Drinkwater's first comedy, *Bird in Hand*. Her stage sweetheart was Laurence Olivier.

During the next two years she accepted whatever came along, appearing in a number of London's small theatres, before making her West End debut in the one-line part of Betty, the serving-maid, in a revival of Nigel Playfair's production of Congreve's *The Way of the World*, in which she also understudied Edith Evans's celebrated Millament.

Her first break came when she was cast as Matheson Lang's leading lady in Ashley Dukes's adaptation of Lion Feuchtwanger's *Jew Süss*. Peggy Ashcroft, amusingly and characteristically self-deprecating, has said that she could not go far wrong in a role which allowed her to read from the *Book of Solomon* and leap to her death by jumping off a balcony backwards when her virtue was threatened. Harold Hobson, watching her performance and listening to 'her voice of unimaginable beauty', was in no doubt that he was in the presence of a major actress. She then went on to be Paul Robeson's leading lady playing Desdemona to his Othello, and once again the simplicity and sincerity of her acting made a deep impression.

During the next fifteen months she appeared in Somerset Maugham's *The Breadwinner*; four drawing-room comedies, the staple diet of the West End theatre, none of them successful; *Hassan* and *Romeo and Juliet* for the Oxford University Dramatic Society; and a one-night stand of Fernand Crommelynck's *Le Cocu Magnifique*, a brutal tragi-farce, in which a husband is so keen to have evidence of his wife's infidelity that he forces her to prostitute herself with their neighbours, who queue up, on camp stools, for her favours.

In 1931, at the age of twenty-four, she became the Old Vic Company's leading lady, and within the space of nine months was seen in no less than ten major roles: Shakespeare's Imogen, Rosalind, Perdita, Portia, Juliet and Miranda, Shaw's Cleopatra, Goldsmith's Kate Hardcastle, John Drinkwater's Mary Stuart and Sheridan's Lady Teazle. She also found time, in the middle of the season, to appear for the Little Theatre in Schnitzler's *Fräulein Elsa*, a role twice as long as Hamlet.

There wasn't much time to do more than learn the lines and get the plays on ('A killing venture, quite beyond my scope at the time, and I knew it,' she was to say later) yet what comes across vividly in the critical reviews of the day is her beauty, charm, delicacy, grace and the freshness of her acting. 'She does not know what it means to use a "trick",' wrote Harcourt Williams in *Old Vic Saga*. 'She has an eye for line and colour and instinctively rejects the commonplace.' Harcourt Williams, who was the Old Vic Company's artistic director, defined her technique as 'absolute honesty and freedom from any suspicion of false sentiment'. It is a technique which has informed her whole career.

Once the season was over she joined the German actor, Werner Krauss, in Gerard Hauptman's *Before Sunset*, a production chiefly remembered for its first night when anti-Nazi demonstrators interrupted the performance. She was then seen in *The Golden Toy*, by Carl Zuckmayer, only remembered for its spectacular awfulness. This was followed by *The Life That I Gave Him*, a little-known one-act play by Pirandello, originally written for Eleanora Duse but never performed by her, and a tour of Beverley Nichols's *Mesmer*, which did not come into London.

Her next role was to have been Lucie Manette in an adaptation of a *Tale of Two Cities*, by John Gielgud and Terence Rattigan, until Martin Harvey, who had been playing Sydney Carton in *The Only Way*, off and on for the previous thirty-six years, complained, saying that their production would jeopardise the success of his farewell tour. So the Dickens was cancelled and she found herself instead being wooed by two Romeos, for this was the famous occasion on which Gielgud and Olivier alternated the lead role and Mercutio.

Gielgud's production of *Romeo and Juliet*, which ran for 189 performances at the New Theatre, breaking all records for a play by Shakespeare, was a milestone in her career. W. A. Darlington, writing in the *Daily Telegraph*, described her as 'the finest and sweetest Juliet of our time'. She was also the youngest, her beauty, sincerity, naturalness and the way she spoke the verse once again making an unforgettable impression on all who saw her. For many, she was, and still is, the definitive Juliet.

One milestone was followed immediately by another when she was cast as Nina in *The Seagull*, the first full-scale production of a Chekhov play in the West End, directed by Theodore Komisarjevsky, one of the great influences in her career.

After spending nine months in America in Maxwell Anderson's verse drama whimsy, *High Tor*, as a three-hundred-year-old ghost, she returned to London to join John Gielgud in his 1937/8 Queen's Theatre season. Her roles included the Queen in *Richard II*, Lady Teazle in Sheridan's *The School for Scandal* (the production was thought to be something of a scandal by those who did not care for director Tyrone Guthrie's innovations and stylised elaborations), Irina in Chekhov's *Three Sisters* and Portia in *The Merchant of Venice*, where her youth was a welcome change from the languid, middle-aged actresses who used to play the Belmont heiress.

The highlight of the season was *Three Sisters*, directed by Michel Saint-Denis, another major influence. The play was rehearsed for eight weeks, an unheard-of period of time in the 1930s, which allowed for an extraordinary attention to detail. The finished result was not only performances of the greatest individual subtlety and sensitivity but also the finest ensemble playing yet seen in England. A. E. Wilson, writing in the *Star*, hailed the production as 'one of the richest experiences London has ever offered or is likely to offer'; and certainly London would have to wait another twenty years for the Moscow Arts Theatre's season of Chekhov plays and Olivier's all-star *Uncle Vanya* for something comparable.

The successful New and Queen's Theatre seasons (a National Theatre, in embryo, for which Gielgud, in the post-War years, has been given far too little credit) led directly to Michel Saint-Denis's Phoenix Theatre season, which was backed by Bronson Albery, a commercial management. Audiences were promised plays by Shakespeare, Chekhov, Molière, Ibsen and Lorca, acted by a company of players, and not the usual *ad hoc* cast, as was, and still is, standard West End practice.

The season opened with *The White Guard*, by the Russian playwright Michael Bulgakov, which proved caviar to the general and was quickly withdrawn, to be replaced by a disappointing *Twelfth Night* (without the promised Edith Evans, Laurence Olivier and Ralph Richardson) and which neither Michael Redgrave as Sir Andrew Aguecheek, nor Peggy Ashcroft as Viola, could save.

Early in 1939 she was seen on tour in Stephen Haggard's anti-Nazi play, *Weep for the Spring*, which did not come into London, then in August she appeared as Cecily Cardew in a major revival of *The Importance of Being Earnest*, bringing to Wilde's comedy, what the director John Gielgud has described as 'a delicious Alice-in-Wonderland-like innocence'. The intention had been to follow the Wilde with Chekhov's *The Cherry Orchard* and Jean Cocteau's *Les Parents Terribles*, but the outbreak of war closed all the London theatres, and by the time Peggy Ashcroft next played in *The Cherry Orchard*, she was old enough to play Mme Ranevsky.

Her plays in the early 1940s included Clemence Dane's *Cousin Muriel*, a poor vehicle for a miscast Edith Evans, in which she and Alec Guinness were young lovers; *The Tempest*, at the Old Vic, in which she took over Miranda from Jessica Tandy; a revival of *The Importance of Being Earnest*; and Rodney Ackland's *The Dark River*, a mock-Chekhovian piece, all futile longing, gratuitous gloom and very little story, set during the Spanish Civil War, in which she played a woman torn between an ineffectual husband and an over-earnest architect. ('How unhappy I could be with neither', said one wag.) Her lambent charm and emotional sincerity were not enough to save the play. A more interesting role would have been Natalia in Turgenev's *A Month in the Country* which she had just begun to rehearse, when she sprained her ankle and had to withdraw from the cast.

Towards the end of the War, she joined John Gielgud in his Haymarket Theatre season, appearing in *Hamlet*, *A Midsummer Night's Dream* and *The Duchess of Malfi*. Her Ophelia, Titania and Duchess were much admired, though there were some critics who did not think she yet had the power for Webster's tragedy. The Duchess (the part she had most wanted to play of the three) would be a role to which she would return fifteen years later.

Towards the end of the 1940s she starred in two highly successful West End plays. Robert Morley and Noel Langley's *Edward, My Son*, in which she played a young woman who ends up as a middle-aged dypsomaniac, was an important stage in her career because it was the first part to break the *ingenue* mould in which she had been cast for so long. In a potentially mawkish part, she was never maudlin; and her acting, too, of the painfully shy and gauche Catherine Sloper, in an adaptation of Henry James's *The Heiress*, so cruelly treated by her father and lover, was equally honest: a performance of delicate insight and pathos.

She made her first appearance at the Memorial Theatre, Stratford-upon-Avon, in 1950, as Beatrice in *Much Ado About Nothing*, and as Cordelia in King Lear. It was difficult to imagine the reconciliation scene between the old king and his daughter being more movingly acted. And as for her Beatrice (one of her finest Shakespearian roles) it was obvious that it must have been a pretty intellectual star which had danced when she was born. She and John Gielgud, as Benedict, were perfectly matched, and such was the popularity of his production, they would be fighting 'the merry war' again five years later.

When the Old Vic Theatre re-opened in 1951 (it had been bombed during the Second World War) her Viola in *Twelfth Night* was greeted like an old friend. Alan Dent, writing in the *News Chronicle*, was as love-sick as any man in Illyria: 'With her flower-like grace and birdlike eloquence – I have all week been in a state of breathless adoration.'

Her next role was a rare opportunity to act in Greek tragedy. Sophocles's *Electra* was a major development in her career, and the experience of having done it, would prove incalculable when she came to play Cleopatra and Margaret of Anjou. The Old Vic season ended with *The Merry Wives of Windsor*, in which she was cast as Mistress Ford.

Neither the Lord Chamberlain (nor Aunt Edna, for that matter) would have approved of the original

3 Hedda in *Hedda Gabler* 1954 ▷

version of Terence Rattigan's *The Deep Blue Sea*. In the early 1950s plays on homosexual themes were still banned and performed only in club theatres. So Rattigan rewrote the leading role, an older man with an obsession for a younger man, for an actress, and offered it to Peggy Ashcroft, who having no sympathy for the woman, turned the part down. Fortunately 'Binkie' Beaumont, the West End manager, who was producing the play, persuaded her to change her mind. She enjoyed one of her biggest successes as Hester Collyer; *The Deep Blue Sea* finally put paid to all those sweet, romantic heroines, at odds with fate and the world, with which she had been identified since the beginning of the 1930s.

In 1953 she was back at Stratford-upon-Avon, in two productions, with Michael Redgrave: first *The Merchant of Venice*, playing Portia, for the third and last time, charming Bassanio and audiences alike with her grace, wit and depth of feeling, and then in *Antony and Cleopatra*.

When it was announced she would be playing Cleopatra, there was considerable surprise, the general concensus being that she was an exquisite miniaturist and that exquisite miniaturists did not play the Serpent of Old Nile. However, once the production was on, though there was, almost inevitably, division among the critics ('Cleopatra from Sloane Square' was Kenneth Tynan's predictable headline in the *Evening Standard*), most were amazed at just how much of the part she had achieved. Peggy Ashcroft has described Cleopatra as one of the most exciting and rewarding roles she has ever played, and one of her happiest times in the theatre.

The following year she played in *Hedda Gabler*. For most people, she was the definitive Hedda of the 1950s. Her originality was to play Ibsen, not as had been expected for tragedy, but for mordant high comedy. The wheedling, bullying, and exasperation with her husband, his aunt and his slippers, were all acted with sharp and merciless irony. The performance, universally praised at home and abroad, was awarded the King's Gold Medal by King Haakon of Norway.

She then appeared as Miss Madrigal, the reprieved murderer, in Enid Bagnold's *The Chalk Garden*, a play originally turned down by every West End management, and not staged in London, until it had been produced successfully in New York. She cut right through the artificial story to provide an over-flowery text with some much-needed potash and granular pest.

Peggy Ashcroft always has had a social and artistic conscience about what the theatre should be doing, and it was no surprise, therefore, that she should be among the first to join George Devine, in the newly-formed English Stage Company, at the Royal Court Theatre, in the first full-scale production of a play by Bertolt Brecht in English. *The Good Woman of Setzuan* (in which she played both a prostitute and a male entrepreneur) arrived in the wake of the Berliner Ensemble's visit to London, in a memorable season, which was to have an immediate effect on British directors and playwrights.

In 1959 she returned to Stratford to play Rosalind in *As You Like It* and Imogen in *Cymbeline*. Since she was now fifty, older than Edith Evans had been when she first assayed Rosalind, there was much comment in the Press on her perennial youthfulness. This was nothing new; her perennial youthfulness always has been commented on (as early as 1938, in fact) and is still, very rightly, being commented on to this day.

She appeared in the West End, in *Shadow of Heroes*, Robert Ardrey's semi-documentary about the Hungarian uprising, and then, for the English Stage Company, in Ibsen's *Rosmersholm*. Rebecca West is not such a showy part as Hedda Gabler, and there were those who would have preferred her to have given a less naturalistic reading of an ambivalent text, and hammed it up a bit, especially in the melodramatic last act; but this has never been her style.

Back at Stratford she found a new way to play two scolds, Katharina in *The Taming of the Shrew* and Paulina in *The Winter's Tale*, before coming to London, in the company's first season at the Aldwych Theatre, with *The Duchess of Malfi*, where she was, without question, the jewel in the Tussaud Laureate's abbatoir. She also appeared in *The Hollow Crown*, John Barton's popular entertainment about the kings and queens of England, with which she would later tour Europe and Canada.

In 1961 the Shakespeare Memorial Theatre Company became the Royal Shakespeare Company and Peter Hall, the new artistic director, needing a star who would be happy to work in an ensemble, invited her to become the first associate artist. The RSC has been Peggy Ashcroft's 'home' ever since, and later she would become one of the company's directors.

Her immediate roles were Emelia in *Othello*, which had a first night unlikely to be forgotten either by the actors or the audience, Ranevsky in an over-broad production of Chekhov's *The Cherry Orchard*, directed by Michel Saint-Denis, and Margaret in *The Wars of the Roses*, a three-part history cycle, drawn from the three *Henry VI* plays and *Richard III*. The production, directed by Peter Hall, has passed into theatrical legend and belongs to the days when John Barton would re-arrange, re-write and *write* Shakespeare. Margaret of Anjou, She-Wolf and indomitable Fury had, for her, all the excitement of playing a new Shakespearian role. It was a magnificent, harrowing portrait, painted on a large scale, and notable for its emotional, physical and vocal authority.

In between the Stratford and London seasons of *The Wars of the Roses* she was with the English Stage Company playing Arkadina to Peter Finch's Trigorin in Chekhov's *The Seagull*, the tantrums being acted at times, almost for farce.

Back with the RSC, she concentrated mainly on modern writing, appearing in a number of complex plays: the mother in Marguerite Duras's *Days in the Trees*, consuming vast amounts of food, hungry for the love of her gigolo son; Mrs Alving in a muted revival of Ibsen's *Ghosts*; and as Agnes in *A Delicate Balance*, by Edward Albee, an author who does not always make it easy either for his actors or his audiences; and this particular piece, occasionally echoing T. S. Eliot and Samuel Beckett, had an enormous sub-text, which the cast had difficulty in discovering. Much better and far more accessible, yet curiously under-rated, was Albee's *All Over*, a death-ritual, written and acted with great style. In both plays she was cast as deeply wounded and deeply embittered wives, who walked the edge of their abysses with wit and detachment.

In the late 1960s and early 1970s she was seen as Beth in Harold Pinter's *Landscape*, Katharine of Aragon in *Henry VIII*, and as a famous communist stage director's wife in Gunter Grass's *The Plebians Rehearse the Uprising*. Beth, the housekeeper, was a role, for which she had particular affection, and she would return to its gentle and haunting beauty four years later, in a double-bill with Pinter's black comedy, *A Slight Ache*.

Outside the RSC, she appeared, for the English Stage Company, in Marguerite Duras's *The Lovers of Viorne*, as a real-life murderer, who had chopped her victim into little pieces and fed them to passing trains. She also appeared in the West End, with Ralph Richardson, in William Douglas Home's *Lloyd George Knew My Father*, though why she should choose such a trivial comedy for her only return to the commercial theatre in sixteen years, was not clear. Similar surprise would be expressed when she and Anthony Quayle appeared, for the RSC, in a trite Soviet matinee play, *Old World*, by Aleksei Arbuzov.

In 1975 she joined Peter Hall, at the National Theatre at the Old Vic, and was seen in his productions of Ibsen's *John Gabriel Borkman* and Samuel Beckett's *Happy Days*. Ibsen's psychological and symbolic drama, in which she was reunited with Ralph Richardson and Wendy Hiller, was a chilling confrontation of obdurates. Her fine performance as Winnie, right up to her neck in it (one of Beckett's least forgettable visual images and metaphors) was a tragi-comic study of indomitable courage in the face of *life*. When the National Theatre moved to their new base, on the South Bank, she played Winnie again, and was also seen in Lilian Hellman's *Watch on the Rhine*, a propaganda piece, designed to get the United States into the Second World War, which was not really worth reviving.

Her last stage performance, directed by Trevor Nunn at Stratford and in the RSC's new London home, at the Barbican, was the Countess of Rousillon in *All's Well That Ends Well*, a play much admired by Bernard Shaw and very few others. Shaw has described the Countess as 'the most beautiful old woman's part ever written'; and certainly, with Peggy Ashcroft acting her, radiating benevolence and good sense, it was very easy to believe she was.

△ 5 Mrs Moore in *A Passage to India* 1984

There is a story that Peggy Ashcroft, at the beginning of her career, was told that if she wanted to act in films she would have to have her nose straightened and her teeth fixed, and though the story *is* true, the real truth is that she preferred to act in the theatre. The theatre was where she felt she belonged.

Her first film was *The Wandering Jew*, in which she played the prostitute who betrays the Jew to the Inquisition. Later she would be seen in a number of critical and popular successes, albeit in small roles, working for such directors as Alfred Hitchcock in *The Thirty-Nine Steps*, Anthony Asquith in *Quiet Wedding*, Fred Zinneman in *The Nun's Story*, Joseph Losey in *Secret Ceremony*, John Schlesinger in *Sunday, Bloody Sunday*, and James Ivory in *Hullabaloo Over George and Bonnie's Pictures*, her one leading role.

For much the same reason that she rejected the large screen, so she rejected the small screen. Her television appearances, in the 1960s and 1970s, were all in productions of plays she had performed either for the RSC or in the West End, and it wasn't until she was cast as Queen Mary in the serial, *Edward and Mrs Simpson*, that she came to the attention of the general public.

Her major break-through was in 1981 when she was seen in two plays, within a week of each other, in two widely differing roles, in Stephen Poliakoff's *Caught on a Train* and Dennis Potter's *Cream in My Coffee*.

Caught on a Train offered her one of her best roles: Frau Messner, the born survivor, was as unforgettable as Barbie Batchelor, the tragic outsider, in Paul Scott's *The Jewel in the Crown*, heart-breaking in her pathos. Barbie, in thirteen weeks on the box, was seen by more people than had seen her act, in six decades, in the theatre – an irony, which was not lost on Peggy Ashcroft herself.

So, just when performing night after night on a stage was beginning, perhaps, to prove a bit difficult, she found a new career in television and films; her seventies have proved an Indian summer with *Hullabaloo over George and Bonnie's Pictures*, *The Jewel in the Crown* and David Lean's *A Passage to India*, for which she won an Oscar as Mrs Moore.

The Oscar, which gave a great deal of pleasure to a great number of people, was seen, by many, to be an award, not just for one performance, in one film, but an award for a lifetime's distinguished work.

Peggy Ashcroft's passion for the theatre is matched only by her passion for political causes (and, of course, cricket). Her commitment to supporting individuals against tyranny is absolute, and she has spoken out on human rights, taking part in demonstrations, vigils, organising petitions and raising money. Campaigner and tireless letter-writer, she has protested against injustices committed in Russia, South Africa, Greece and elsewhere. She has done many poetry recitals on behalf of Amnesty International and in support of the magazine, *Index on Censorship*, often giving her voice to poets whose works might not otherwise be heard. And she has done all this without ever exploiting her career for the causes she espouses.

Peggy Ashcroft, the least actressy of actresses, unaffected, unpretentious, essentially private, has been the supreme actress of our time, a positive influence in every company she has been in, a star yet an ensemble player, who always puts the play and the production before herself.

Equally adept in tragedy and comedy, she has played an extraordinary range of parts with subtlety and versatility. Her intellectual and emotional grasp of character, the economy and truth of her acting, and its total lack of sentimentality and artifice, the beauty and musicality of her voice, her consummate technical skill – all these qualities have long been recognised and admired by the acting profession and her audiences.

The pages which follow are a record of her career. They are also a tribute to a woman, whose warmth and integrity, loyalty and commitment, vulnerability and humility, have made her one of the best-loved actresses of our time.

6 Naemi in *Jew Süss* 1929 ▷

The 1920s

7 *The Merchant of Venice*   1920

Peggy Ashcroft as Portia in Shakespeare's *The Merchant of Venice*,
directed by Gwen Lally at Woodford School, Croydon.

By the time Peggy Ashcroft was thirteen, she knew she wanted
to be an actress. Gwen Lally encouraged her love of Shakespeare,
and amongst the roles she acted at Woodford School were
Shylock, Brutus, Celia, and Katharine in *Henry V*.

Portia was a role to which she would return at drama school in
1926, at the Old Vic in 1932, at the Queen's Theatre in 1938,
and at the Memorial Theatre, Stratford-upon-Avon, in 1953.

8 *Bird in Hand   1927*

Percy Rhodes, Carrie Baillie, Frank Rendall, Charles Maunsell, Ivor Bernard, Laurence Olivier and Peggy Ashcroft in John Drinkwater's *Bird in Hand*, directed by the author at the Birmingham Repertory Theatre.

Peggy Ashcroft played the village innkeeper's daughter who wants to marry the squire's son, but her father does not believe that girls should marry above their station.

Miss Peggy Ashcroft's Joan Greenleaf was a charming, sensible, staightforward impersonation. The part, naturally drawn, was naturally acted.

Birmingham Post

9 *Jew Süss* 1929

Matheson Lang as Joseph Süss Oppenheimer and Peggy Ashcroft
as Naemi in Ashley Dukes's adaptation of Lion Feuchtwanger's
historical romance, *Jew Süss*, directed by Matheson Lang and
Reginald Denham at the Duke of York's Theatre.

Naemi commits suicide when her virtue is threatened. The
sincerity and integrity of Peggy Ashcroft's acting was thrown into
high relief by what *The Times* described as 'the lavish emotional
display of Matheson Lang, all magnetic eyes and thrilling
tremelo'.

*But perhaps, the most attractive performance of all was that of Peggy
Ashcroft, a young actress of whom I had not before heard. She acted
the part of Naemi, the Jew's daughter, with a proud innocence that was
exquisitely lovely.*

St John Ervine *Observer*

10 Juliet in *Romeo and Juliet* 1935 ▷

The 1930s

11 Othello 1930

Paul Robeson as Othello and Peggy Ashcroft as Desdemona in
Shakespeare's *Othello*, directed by Ellen van Volkenburg at the
Savoy Theatre.

Peggy Ashcroft was asked to audition for Desdemona as a
direct result of Paul Robeson seeing her performance in *Jew Süss*.
The simplicity and sincerity she had brought to Feuchtwanger's
romantic melodrama she now brought to her first professional
Shakespearian role.

*Miss Peggy Ashcroft's Desdemona was beautiful beyond qualification
and lacked nothing in tenderness and dignity.*

Ivor Brown *Manchester Guardian*

*By this performance she establishes her reputation, already fairly won,
as a most promising actress.*

W. A. Darlington *Daily Telegraph*

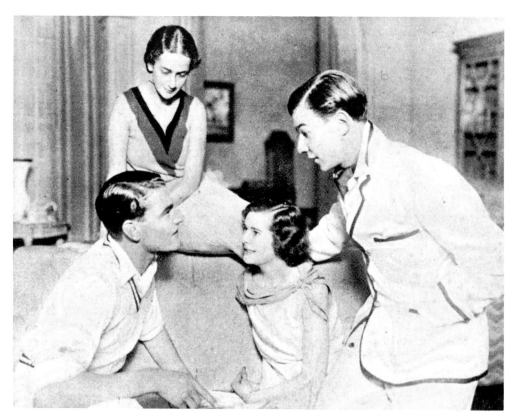

12 *The Breadwinner* *1930*

Marie Löhr as Margery Battle, Evelyn Roberts as Alfred Granger,
Ronald Squire as Charles Battle, Peggy Ashcroft as Judy Battle
and Jack Hawkins as Patrick Battle in W. Somerset Maugham's
The Breadwinner, directed by Athole Stewart at the Vaudeville
Theatre.

Maugham's cynical comedy is about a stockbroker father
walking out on his awful family and their outrage at finding they
mean as little to him as he does to them.

Peggy Ashcroft played the daughter, a Bright Young Thing, a
role which allowed for an effective *volte face* in the third act when
the girl is found to be fundamentally decent underneath all the
facetiousness and callousness.

One of her best lines ('Don't you know that since the war the
amateurs have entirely driven the professionals out of business?
No girl can make a decent living now by prostitution') was
quoted so much by the gentlemen of the Press that it was cut after
the first night, the management anticipating, rightly, that the
Lord Chamberlain would shortly be paying the theatre a visit.

13 *Hassan* *1931*

Raymond Raikes as Rafi, Peggy Ashcroft as Pervaneh and George
Devine as the Caliph in James Elroy Flecker's *Hassan*, directed by
Gibson Cowan for the Oxford University Dramatic Society.

14 *Charles the 3rd* *1931*

Cecil Humphreys as Petrops and Peggy Ashcroft as Angela in
Curt Götz's *Charles the 3rd*, directed by Mrs Edgar Wallace at
Wyndham's Theatre.

Angela is a novice who, when falsely charged with
disobedience and unchastity, tries to drown herself. *The Times*
described Peggy Ashcroft's performance as a 'lovely miniature',
but did not care for the script: 'Seldom have phrases been hewn
out of stone with a blunter or more self-conscious chisel.'

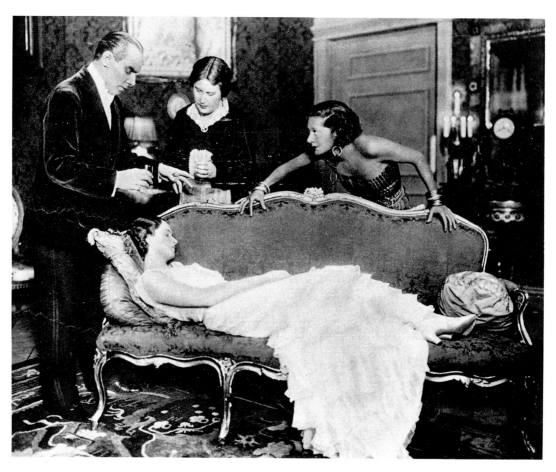

15 *Take Two From One* 1931

Nicholas Hannen, Olga Slade, Gertrude Lawrence and Peggy Ashcroft in Gregorio and Maria Martinez Sierra's *Take Two From One*, directed by Theodore Komisarjevsky at the Theatre Royal, Haymarket.

Take Two From One was an inconsequential farce about two women fighting over one embarrassed husband. Gertrude Lawrence played the tempestuous first wife, presumed dead, who returns home, having spent two years in the African jungle. Peggy Ashcroft played the second and much meeker wife. It was a role which allowed her to be amusingly angelic.

It is what she is as well as her marvellous professionalism which makes Peggy a great actress and a wonderful person with whom to collaborate. The first time we designed her costumes was for her Juliet in the OUDS production. Since then she has worn many of our designs, without vanity but with real style and appreciation and always a deep understanding of how to use them to help the interpretation of the character.

Motley

16 *Romeo and Juliet* 1932

Christopher Hassall as Romeo and Peggy Ashcroft as Juliet in Shakespeare's *Romeo and Juliet*, directed by John Gielgud for the Oxford University Dramatic Society.

It had always been Peggy Ashcroft's dream to play Juliet. The cast included Edith Evans as the Nurse, George Devine, the then-president of the OUDS, as Mercutio, and an indifferent undergraduate actor called Terence Rattigan, who was so bad that what few lines he had as the musician were taken away from him.

This production was John Gielgud's first-ever and, with hindsight, can be seen as a first sketch for his famous 1935 New Theatre production.

And above all this Juliet is in love – not rehearsing phrases, but passionately in love. The high music of that love's despair sometimes tests her too far, but its melancholy is a rapture and its delights are delight itself.

The Times

17 *The Secret Woman* 1932

Nancy Price as Ann Redvers and Peggy Ashcroft as Salome Westaway in Eden Phillpotts's *The Secret Woman*, a Dartmoor tragedy, directed by Nancy Price.

18 *Caesar and Cleopatra* 1932

Peggy Ashcroft as Cleopatra in George Bernard Shaw's *Caesar and Cleopatra*, directed by Harcourt Williams for the Old Vic Company.

At twenty-four, Peggy Ashcroft became the Old Vic's Company's leading lady. Her Cleopatra was a petulant mixture of minx and kitten.

It was an innovation for the Old Vic, the home of Shakespeare, to put on a play by Shaw. Such was the applause on the first night that Lilian Baylis, founder of the Old Vic and Sadler's Wells, said she felt quite jealous for Shakespeare's reputation.

Miss Peggy Ashcroft received the kind of welcome the outer world reserves for visiting Hollywood stars, and the Old Vic for the apple of its eye.

Harold Hobson *Observer*

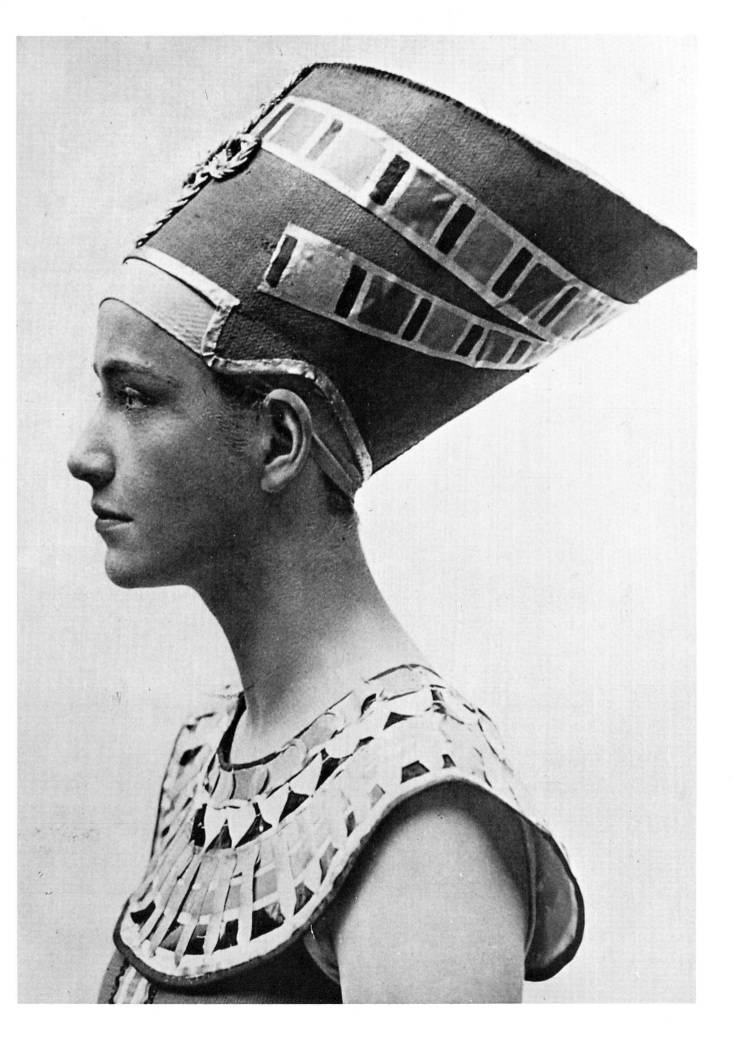

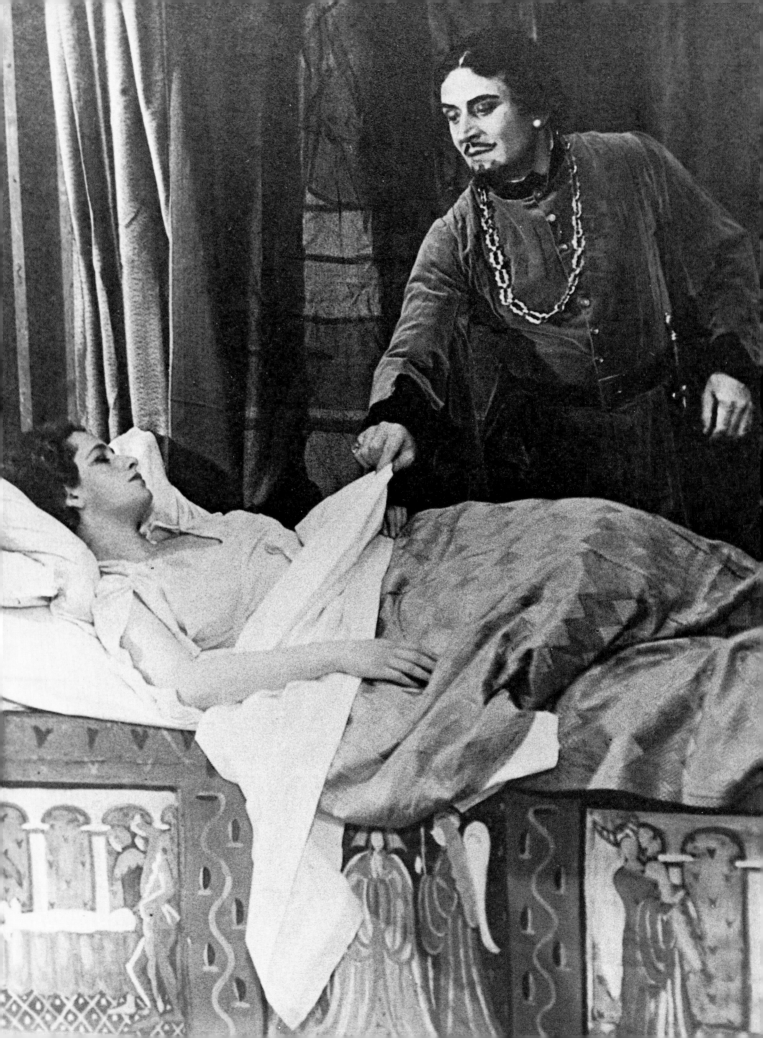

19 Cymbeline 1932

Peggy Ashcroft as Imogen and Malcolm Keen as Iachimo in Shakespeare's *Cymbeline*, directed by Harcourt Williams for the Old Vic Company.

Cymbeline is not a play which is done very often and perhaps the only way to achieve the sort of success it had in the last century would be to give the story the full Rossetti-like Medieval Romance. Harcourt Williams's production was an unsatisfactory compromise between Boccacio and *Snow White and the Seven Dwarfs*. When audiences stayed away Lilian Baylis, somewhat unfairly, harangued those who had come.

20 As You Like It 1932

Valerie Tudor as Celia, Peggy Ashcroft as Rosalind, Geoffrey Wincott as Touchstone and Marius Goring as Le Beau in Shakespeare's *As You Like It*, directed by Harcourt Williams for the Old Vic Company.

Miss Peggy Ashcroft was the Rosalind, and that young lady gave us all that is left after taking away the poetry, the depth of feeling, and what I should like to call the lineage of the part. Rosalind is sister to Beatrice, and in other ages would be Millament and Clara Middleton. In plain words, she must have style. Miss Ashcroft made her a nice little girl in a wood.

James Agate *Sunday Times*

21 Fräulein Elsa 1932

Peggy Ashcroft as Elsa in Arthur Schnitzler's *Fräulein Elsa*,
adapted and directed by Theodore Komisarjevsky for the
Independent Theatre Club at the Kingsway Theatre.

Elsa is one of the longest parts ever written for an actress. Peggy
Ashcroft gave a poignant performance as the young and innocent
girl who violates her modesty to save her father from bankruptcy,
and suffers a mental breakdown.

The play was banned by the Lord Chamberlain, largely
because of a scene in which Elsa removes her clothes in a hotel
foyer. The Independent Theatre Club was formed to circumvent
the ban.

The nudity was simulated: wearing a stole and a dress with a
bare-back, Peggy Ashcroft, facing up-stage, collapsed to the
floor, as the stole slipped off her shoulders.

22 The Merchant of Venice 1932

Charles Hickman as Bassanio, Peggy Ashcroft as Portia, Valerie
Tudor as Jessica, William Fox as Lorenzo, Cecil Winterbottom as
Antonio, Patricia McNab as Nerissa and Roger Livesey as
Gratiano in Shakespeare's *The Merchant of Venice*, directed by
John Gielgud for the Old Vic Company.

John Gielgud fantasticated the story of Portia and her suitors to
throw the realism of Shylock and his debtor into high relief. He
simplified the setting and instead of lowering the curtain between
scenes, as was then the usual practice, lowered it only at the
interval. The production was dressed in a variety of periods.
Today this is the norm with the Royal Shakespeare Company
but, in the early 1930s, it was thought to smack too much of a
Cochrane revue.

*Miss Peggy Ashcroft's Portia was a lively, witty, sophisticated,
mischievous maid, quite capable of conceiving and almost of carrying
through her pretty prank. The 'quality of mercy' speech was not given
as a purple patch, but almost in a confidential tone, hands behind back
– theoretically no doubt a quite indefensible reading, but surprisingly
effective.*

Joseph Thorp *Punch*

23 *The Winter's Tale 1933*

William Fox as Florizel and Peggy Ashcroft as Perdita in
Shakespeare's *The Winter's Tale*, directed by Harcourt Williams
for the Old Vic Company.

*Not all the maunderings of Victorian scholarship over Shakespeare's
heroines have power to suggest a Perdita as peerless as Miss Peggy
Ashcroft's. She filled the stage with quick and eager beauty, adroitly
concealing the fact that Shakespeare had given her nothing else to fill it
with.*

Peter Fleming *Spectator*

24 *She Stoops to Conquer*   1933

Valerie Tudor as Constance Neville, Peggy Ashcroft as Kate
Hardcastle, William Fox as Hastings, Charles Hickman as Young
Marlow in Oliver Goldsmith's *She Stoops to Conquer*, directed by
Harcourt Williams for the Old Vic Company.

25 Mary Stuart 1933

Peggy Ashcroft as Mary and Claire Harris
as Mary Beaton in John Drinkwater's
Mary Stuart, directed by Harcourt
Williams for the Old Vic Company.

    John Drinkwater's Mary was a sweet,
unhappy woman, noble and beautiful.
Most people would have much preferred
to have seen the murderess and wanton of
legend rather than a conventional heroine
of romance.

26 Romeo and Juliet 1933

Peggy Ashcroft as Juliet and Marius
Goring as Romeo in Shakespeare's *Romeo
and Juliet*, directed by Harcourt Williams
for the Old Vic Company.

*She has the magic. She has also the experience
and can establish that transition from piping
innocence to the full-throated cry of the
tragedienne which has always made Juliet's
part so sharp a test of dramatic scope and
range.*

Ivor Brown *Observer*

27 The School for Scandal 1933

Malcolm Keen as Sir Peter Teazle, William Fox as Sir Benjamin
Backbite, Veronica Turnleigh as Lady Sneerwell, Peggy Ashcroft
as Lady Teazle, Clare Harris as Mrs Candour and Alistair Sim as
Crabtree in Richard Brinsley Sheridan's *The School for Scandal*,
directed by Harcourt Williams for the Old Vic Company.

Sir Peter Teazle enjoys his 'daily jangle' with his wife almost as
much as the audience does: 'With what charming air she
contradicts everything I say and how pleasantly she shows her
contempt.'

Peggy Ashcroft's vivacious Lady Teazle was a charmer,
elegantly mannered and beautifully spoken.

28 The Tempest 1933

Peggy Ashcroft as Miranda and Harcourt Williams as Prospero in
Shakespeare's *The Tempest*, directed by Harcourt Williams for
the Old Vic Company.

*Miss Peggy Ashcroft's Miranda speaks as though her lines were newly
minted.*

Harold Hobson *Observer*

29 Before Sunset 1933

Werner Krauss and Peggy Ashcroft in Gerhardt Hauptmann's
Before Sunset, directed by Miles Malleson at the Shaftesbury
Theatre.

Werner Krauss, the distinguished German actor, played an
elderly widower, whose family seeks to put him in an asylum,
when he decides to marry a girl, who is fifty years his junior and
his social inferior.

The first night was chiefly memorable for its stormy reception
by anti-Nazi demonstrators, who showered the auditorium with
leaflets, which said: 'A message to Hitler through Werner Krauss.
We want British actors for British plays. Not Nazi-actors.
Boycott Hitler. Buy British.'

Peggy Ashcroft had to make a direct appeal to the audience
before the cast was able to continue.

*Miss Ashcroft suggested the girl's devotion and innocence and hero-
worship with beautiful discretion, giving the part its warmth and saving
it from weak prettiness.*

The Times

30 *The Wandering Jew* 1933

Peggy Ashcroft as Olalla Quintana in the film version of E.
Temple Thurston's play, *The Wandering Jew*, directed by Maurice
Elvey.

Conrad Veidt played the Jew and Peggy Ashcroft, making her
screen debut, the prostitute who unwittingly betrays him to the
Inquisition. The film was re-edited and re-released in 1939 as
A People Eternal.

31 *The Golden Toy* *1934*

Ion Swinley as Karudatta and Peggy Ashcroft as Vasantesena in Carl Zuckmayer's *The Golden Toy*, directed by Ludwig Berger at the Coliseum Theatre.

   The Golden Toy, based on an old Indian legend, relates the adventures of a young prince, who is kidnapped at birth, a butcher's son having been substituted for him in his cradle. He falls in love with Vasantesena, a temple dancing-girl.

   Five hundred people were employed in making costumes and scenery for a cast which numbered two hundred. The Coliseum's triple revolving stage was used for the first time. There was music by Schumann, a baby elephant and some incongruous music hall comedy. The end result was spectacularly awful.

32 *The Life That I Gave Him* *1934*

Peggy Ashcroft as Lucia Maubel and Nancy Price as Donna Anna Luna in Luigi Pirandello's *The Life That I Gave Him*, directed by Frank Birch at the Little Theatre.

33 *Romeo and Juliet* 1935

Peggy Ashcroft as Juliet and Laurence Olivier as Romeo in
Shakespeare's *Romeo and Juliet*, directed by John Gielgud at the
New Theatre.

34 *Romeo and Juliet* 1935

Peggy Ashcroft as Juliet and Laurence Olivier as Romeo in
Shakespeare's *Romeo and Juliet*.

*Dame Peggy is, as she has always been, a brilliantly true artist without
a second of anything that is not entirely and wonderfully honest in her
work.*

*I have, of course, followed her career with the most intense interest
ever since 1924, when we were fellow students.*

*I suppose, if I could qualify this in any way, it might add a little
interest to otherwise somewhat vapid comments, but when one has
nothing but praise for an actor (or actress, though, I suppose, in
general terms, the first word is the correct one), it is a little difficult to be
anything but specious and possibly, and most improperly, a little
lacking in flame which, indeed, the subject is anything but.*

Laurence Olivier

35 *Romeo and Juliet* 1935

Edith Evans as the Nurse and Peggy Ashcroft as Juliet in Shakespeare's *Romeo and Juliet.*

Peggy Ashcroft was wooed by *two* Romeos, for this was the famous occasion on which John Gielgud and Laurence Olivier alternated Romeo and Mercutio. She has made no secret that she, contrary to the received critical opinion of the day, always thought Olivier was the best Romeo and Gielgud the best Mercutio.

It has often been said that Juliet, because of her traumatic experiences – having sex for the first time, death of Tybalt, banishment of Romeo, secret-marriage, mock-suicide, etc – that she matures overnight. The originality of Peggy Ashcroft's interpretation was that she remained a child throughout; the tragedy was in the girl's heart-stopping youth, an emotional life cut short, just as it was about to begin.

The production was a milestone in her career.

Playgoers who fervently applauded last night will never forget the Juliet of Miss Peggy Ashcroft. It was a flawless miracle.
M. Willson Disher *Daily Mail*

36 *Romeo and Juliet* 1935

John Gielgud as Romeo and Peggy Ashcroft as Juliet in Shakespeare's *Romeo and Juliet.*

Now she gives us the whole portrait. Without losing a trace of the lovely eagerness, and innocence of the earlier scenes, she rises to the tragedy and shows herself to be, what one had always thought she might some day be, the finest as well as the sweetest Juliet of our time.
W. A. Darlington *Daily Telegraph*

Technically her performance is perfection; there is no one like her for conveying the sense of a difficult passage without, so to speak, being caught in the act – without wittingly making us pause to admire her virtuosity. She does more than make Shakespeare's expression of Juliet's thoughts seem natural; she makes it seem inevitable.
Peter Fleming *Spectator*

I cannot imagine a sweeter, sincerer or more melting Juliet. Each word and movement had a kind of sacred rapture. She was every young girl enchanted in the bitter-sweet wisdom of first love.
Stephen Williams *Evening Standard*

37 *The Thirty-Nine Steps* 1935

Robert Donat as Richard Hannay, Peggy Ashcroft as Mrs Crofter and John Laurie as Mr Crofter in the film version of John Buchan's *The Thirty-Nine Steps*, directed by Alfred Hitchcock.

Peggy Ashcroft played the small part of the Scottish crofter's young wife, who helps Richard Hannay to escape before he is either betrayed to the police or murdered by her jealous husband.

Hitchcock was convinced that Peggy Ashcroft had a brilliant career in front of her: 'The greatest thing about her is her extreme simplicity', he said.

38 *Rhodes of Africa* 1936

Walter Houston as Cecil Rhodes and Peggy Ashcroft as Anna Carpenter in *Rhodes of Africa*, a film directed by Berthold Viertel.

Rhodes, a diamond miner, became Prime Minister of Cape Colony. Anna Carpenter was based on the writer Olive Schreiner, pacifist, feminist and socialist, who championed the blacks and was outspokenly critical of his imperialist role.

39 *The Seagull* 1936

John Gielgud as Trigorin and Peggy Ashcroft as Nina in Anton Chekhov's *The Seagull*, directed by Theodore Komisarjevsky at the New Theatre.

40 *The Seagull* 1936

Stephen Haggard as Konstantin and Peggy Ashcroft as Nina in Anton Chekhov's *The Seagull*.

When Chekhov was asked how he would like his play performed he replied he would like it performed as well as possible. Theodore Komisarjevsky's production was, by common consent, one of the great Chekhovian productions of the 1930s.

Young actresses, who play the stage-struck Nina, usually manage the first three acts; it is the difficult last act, which, almost invariably, defeats them.

Miss Ashcroft has done nothing better than her Nina, the part is perfect in its growth from the dewy innocence of the first two acts to the pale, storm-pelted desperation of the last.

Ivor Brown *Observer*

Miss Ashcroft's Nina has an enchanting freshness in the early scenes, and her tragic return has the supreme quality of being indeed not the coming of a stranger but the return of the girl we have known, changed by suffering but not obliterated by it, so that what she was is visible always through what she has become.

The Times

Peggy Ashcroft found in Nina a chance to show again that heart-rending sense of youth at odds with fate which made her Juliet so memorable.

W. A. Darlington *Daily Telegraph*

41 *High Tor* 1937

Peggy Ashcroft as Lise and Burgess Meredith as Van Van Doren
in Maxwell Anderson's *High Tor*, directed by Guthrie McClintic
at the Martin Beck Theatre, New York.

High Tor, a verse drama fantasy, set on a mountain near New
City where Maxwell Anderson lived, was a satire on American
business destroying nature.

Peggy Ashcroft played the ghost of one of the Dutch settlers,
who had come up the Hudson River three hundred years before.

42 *Richard II* 1937

Peggy Ashcroft as Queen, John Gielgud as Richard and Leon
Quartermaine (far right) as John of Gaunt in Shakespeare's
Richard II, directed by John Gielgud at the Queen's Theatre.

43 *The School for Scandal* 1937

John Gielgud as Sir Joseph Surface and Peggy Ashcroft as Lady
Teazle in Richard Brinsley Sheridan's *The School for Scandal*,
directed by Tyrone Guthrie at the Queen's Theatre.

Lady Teazle is an innocent abroad, who, wanting to be
thought a lady of fashion, foolishly compromises herself with Sir
Joseph Surface, only to regret her imprudence, long before the
screen is down.

Sheridan's eighteenth-century mixture of mischief and
sentiment was given such an over-stylised production by Tyrone
Guthrie that many critics felt they were watching a ballet.

*Miss Peggy Ashcroft is the daintiest rogue in porcelain and quarrels to
perfection.*

Ivor Brown *Observer*

*As Lady Teazle Miss Ashcroft is breathless with innocence when she
should be panting under a smother of acquired elegance. Apart from
this her performance is charming.*

James Agate *Sunday Times*

44 *Three Sisters*   *1938*

Peggy Ashcroft as Irina and Michael Redgrave as Tusenbach in Anton Chekhov's *Three Sisters*, directed by Michel Saint-Denis at the Queen's Theatre.

How shall we live our lives? What shall become of us? Life is slipping by and it will never come back.

Chekhov's play is not the tragedy of any one individual, but rather a concerted tragedy, the lines having a choral, even a liturgical effect. The pain and anguish of time passing and unrealised dreams is echoed and reiterated by a group of people who have been cruelly cheated and whose only hope now lies in work and the future.

Michel Saint-Denis's beautifully co-ordinated and orchestrated production was one of the finest examples of ensemble playing yet seen in England. Peggy Ashcroft's Irina was heart-breaking. The contrast between the bubbling, glowing girl of the first two acts, so alive and vital, and the sorrow of the last two, was most movingly acted.

45 *Three Sisters*   *1938*

Peggy Ashcroft as Irina, Gwen Ffrangcon-Davies as Olga and Carol Goodner as Masha in Anton Chekhov's *Three Sisters*.

One should not fling the word 'masterpiece' carelessly about but I am using such terms with all deliberation and consideration. For this is a masterpiece as a dramatic conception, and in the manner of presentation and acting; nothing that I have seen in the theatre for many years has so profoundly moved me, and so burned itself into my memory.

A. E. Wilson *Star*

Anyone who fails to see this production will miss one of the greatest intellectual and aesthetic pleasures the modern theatre can afford.
Rupert Hart-Davis *Spectator*

46 *The Merchant of Venice*
   1938

Peggy Ashcroft as Portia in Shakespeare's
The Merchant of Venice, directed by John
Gielgud at the Queen's Theatre.

*Now that we have seen a proper Portia,
gleaming with adolescent fun and tenderness,
it is to be hoped that callipygian matrons will
abjure the role.*
                New Statesman and Nation

*Belmont is not overwhelmed by Venice and
Portia is permitted to rule in her own country.
Miss Ashcroft rules it with magic, giving
Portia her miraculous youth, her sweetness,
her wise gravity, her underlying spirit of
laughter; carrying the court scene with a
natural ease and humour, converting the
whole part into a lyric and giving to the play a
freshness such as we do not remember having
seen upon it before.*
                The Times

47 *The Merchant of Venice*
   1938

Peggy Ashcroft as Portia in Shakespeare's
The Merchant of Venice.

48 *The White Guard*   1938

Peggy Ashcroft as Yeliena Talberg, Glen Byam Shaw as
Alexander Studsinsky, Michael Redgrave as Alexei Turtin,
Stephen Haggard as Lariossik, Basil C. Langton as Nikolka
Turbin and George Devine as Viktor Myschlajevsky in Michael
Bulgakov's *The White Guard*, directed by Michel Saint-Denis at
the Phoenix Theatre.

    The White Guard traces the fortunes and misfortunes of one
bourgeois family and their friends during the civil war which
followed the Russian Revolution.

    The timing of the production was hardly ideal, coming, as it
did, shortly after the Munich Conference. The public stayed
away and the play was withdrawn after only three weeks and not
seen again until the Royal Shakespeare Company revived it with
great success forty years later.

    The White Guard was said to be one of Stalin's favourite plays.

*Miss Peggy Ashcroft, a leading lady who is not afraid to look untidy,
gives a most moving performance. Yet she is presented by the author
with no character; somehow, and magically, she weaves pathos out of
the void.*

Ivor Brown *Observer*

*Miss Peggy Ashcroft gave an exquisite performance of something which
got no nearer to Russian than the handbag department at Harridges.*

James Agate *Sunday Times*

49 *Twelfth Night*   *1938*

Esmond Knight as Orsino, Peggy Ashcroft as Viola, Vera Lindsay
as Olivia and Basil C. Langton as Sebastian in Shakespeare's
Twelfth Night, directed by Michel Saint-Denis at the Phoenix
Theatre.

Michel Saint-Denis was much criticised for cutting away all
the traditional business and putting nothing in its place, when,
in fact, what he was doing was reproducing Jacques Copeau's
famous 1914 production.

Peggy Ashcroft was praised for the gentleness and truthfulness
of her acting and for the exquisite way she spoke the verse. There
was a charming moment when Viola, forgetting she was disguised
as a boy, and with her master's lady, very nearly cried *Orsino!*
(instead of *Olivia!*) to the reverberate hills, and checked herself
only just in time.

50 *The Tempest* 1939

John Abbott as Prospero, Richard Ainley as Ferdinand and Peggy Ashcroft as Miranda in Shakespeare's *The Tempest* directed by Dallas Bower for BBC Television.

This *Tempest* was the first-ever television production of a Shakespeare play by the BBC from Alexandra Palace.

The airy fairy spirits who melted into thin air by trick photography did less to create the atmosphere of the enchanted isle than did Miss Ashcroft's wide-eyed wonderment.

The Times

51 *Weep for the Spring* 1939

Stephen Haggard as Frederick Bren and Peggy Ashcroft as Isolde in Stephen Haggard's *Weep for the Spring*, directed by Michel Saint-Denis on tour.

Weep for the Spring was set in Nazi Germany. Peggy Ashcroft played a girl engaged to marry a count she does not love, who falls in love with a law student, whose politics are a danger not only to himself but her family. She is forced to give him up. The play was touching, but not quite strong enough, and did not come into London.

52   *The Importance of Being Earnest*   1939

Gwen Ffrangcon-Davies as Gwendolen Fairfax and Peggy
Ashcroft as Cecily Cardew in Oscar Wilde's *The Importance of
Being Earnest*, directed by John Gielgud at the Globe Theatre.

Peggy Ashcroft, as the pretty eighteen-year-old ward, acted
with sophisticated innocence. The famous tea-scene, sweet and
pert, a feline battle of wits, which little Cecily wins game, set and
match, was fought with all the polite rudeness of the well-bred.

*How glad I am to share in the pæon of praise and love to you darling
Peggy on your eightieth birthday. What lovely things we have shared in
the theatre over the years – the fun of the tea-party in* The Importance
– the sorrows and joys of the Three Sisters *– and our joint worship of
Michel Saint-Denis in those inspiring rehearsals – and the last of our
togetherness in the theatre,* King Lear *at Stratford. I used to stand in
the wings to watch you and John in the 'awakening' scene and hear you
say 'no cause, no cause' with such tender love and pity that I had to
move away quickly – the threat of tears did not become the evil Regan I
was to play in the next scene.*

Gwen Ffrangcon-Davies

53 Duchess in *The Duchess of Malfi* 1945 ▷

The 1940s

It is her personal warmth which gets to you; and it has got to me for over fifty years. There is nothing phoney or so-called 'theatrical' about it (she has her dislikes and is not very good at disguising them) but the warmth is just there, emanating from her rich personality. Her laughter, too – which is somehow unexpected in an actress who has made such a great reputation in tragic roles. Her integrity as artist is profound and total. Every performance seems to leave her drained of spirit, but never with a trace of affectation, and often, when I have gone round to see her after a play, I have found her rather crumpled and worn. Except for once, which was after Ibsen's Hedda Gabler. 'You are looking very spry,' I said, 'having seen what you have just gone through.' 'Oh, I'm as bright as a button,' she replied. 'You see, Hedda is heartless and cold. She doesn't tax me emotionally at all. I love playing her. It's like a holiday.'

Alec Guinness

54 *Cousin Muriel* 1940

Peggy Ashcroft as Dinah Sylvester and Alec Guinness as Richard Meilhac in Clemence Dane's *Cousin Muriel*, directed by Norman Marshall at the Globe Theatre.

Cousin Muriel was a cheat, liar, forger and thief. Alec Guinness played her son, unfairly tarred with the same brush, and Peggy Ashcroft was the girl he wanted to marry.

The general feeling was that Edith Evans was miscast in the title role and that the third act did not work at all.

55 *Channel Incident* 1940

Anthony Asquith directs Peggy Ashcroft and Gordon Harker in *Channel Incident*, a Ministry of Information film.

Peggy Ashcroft played a woman who takes her little boat across the Channel to help in the evacuation of Dunkirk. In order to get the necessary supplies from the naval authorities, she first has to disguise herself as a man.

56 *Quiet Wedding 1941*

Peggy Ashcroft as Flower Lisle and Derek Farr as Dallas Chaytor
in the film version of Esther McCracken's stage play, *Quiet
Wedding*, directed by Anthony Asquith.

Derek Farr was the groom and Margaret Lockwood the bride
with the first-night nerves.

Peggy Ashcroft, who had taken over her role from Kay
Hammond at the last minute, was cast as the bride's brother's
tactless fiancée, an awful flirt, who arrives, from London, with a
pet rabbit and one of those piercing, frightfully-English voices.
'You're not going to like me,' she tells her prospective in-laws.

57 *Hamlet 1944*

Peggy Ashcroft as Ophelia in Shakespeare's *Hamlet*, directed by
George Rylands at the Theatre Royal, Haymarket. John Gielgud
was Hamlet.

*Miss Ashcroft's fine temperate vocal pathos contributed to one of the
peaks of the production, the 'Get thee to a nunnery' scene; and she
spoke Ophelia's concluding lament, 'O what a noble mind is here
o'erthrown' with a fastidious truth that lacked only one thing to make it
still more impressive; a longer pause before and after it.*

Desmond MacCarthy *New Statesman and Nation*

58 A Midsummer Night's Dream 1945

Peggy Ashcroft as Titania and John Gielgud as Oberon in
Shakespeare's *A Midsummer Night's Dream*, directed by Nevill
Coghill at the Theatre Royal, Haymarket.

Peggy Ashcroft, a spirit of no common rate, was a bewitching
fairy queen, beautifully light and gently musical.

Most critics were disappointed that Mendelssohn's music had
been dropped and that there was no ballet, though she and
Gielgud did do a little *pas de deux*, specially choreographed for
them by Frederick Ashton.

59 *The Duchess of Malfi* 1945

Joy Harvey as Cariola, Leslie Banks as Bologna and Peggy Ashcroft as the Duchess in John Webster's *The Duchess of Malfi*, directed by George Rylands at the Theatre Royal, Haymarket.

Webster's sombre and decadent melodrama is a horror story in the familiar Jacobean theatre mould; though for an audience, who had just been made aware of the atrocities committed by the Germans at Belsen and other concentration camps, the tortures, the Duchess suffered in this particular production, seemed more decorative than horrible.

Miss Ashcroft's Duchess seems to me the richest thing she has done. A touch more majesty, especially in the opening scene, perhaps? But how lovely, how fresh, how pathetic, how direct!
Raymond Mortimer *New Statesman and Nation*

Miss Ashcroft's Duchess has a true long-suffering majesty along with the beauty of voice and stance; occasionally she wants more range and variety of voice, never more quality of grace.
Ivor Brown *Observer*

Something more than plaintiveness, however touching, is wanted if 'I am Duchess of Malfi still' is not to sound like 'I am still little Miss Muffet'.
James Agate *Sunday Times*

60, 61, 62 *Edward, My Son*   *1947*

Peggy Ashcroft as Evelyn Holt in Robert Morley and Noel
Langley's *Edward, My Son*, directed by Peter Ashmore at His
Majesty's Theatre. The production transferred to the Martin
Beck Theatre, New York, in 1948.

Edward, who is never seen, is the worthless son of a crooked
newspaper magnate, who indulges him. The play, covering a
period of some twenty-eight years from 1919 to 1947, traces the
rise of the father, through arson, blackmail and murder, to the
peerage, and the descent of his wife, through neglect and
disillusionment, to alcoholism.

Robert Morley and Peggy Ashcroft played Edward's parents.
Her role was so unlike the sweet, romantic heroines the public
had identified her with for so long, that her performance took
everybody by surprise.

*It is a long time since we have seen so considered and so imaginative a
piece of acting as hers and whenever she appeared, this clever and
unstable comedy took on a depth and texture which its horrifying
implications demanded.*

New Statesman and Nation

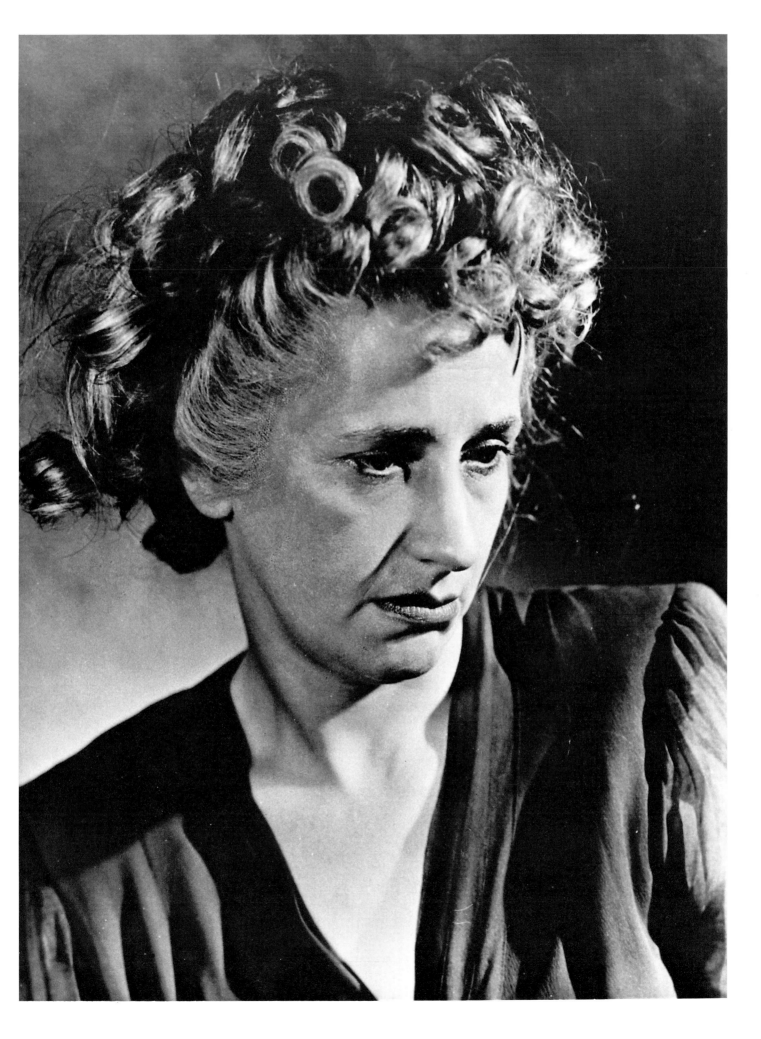

63 *The Heiress* 1949

Peggy Ashcroft as Catherine Sloper and Ralph Richardson as Dr
Sloper in Ruth and Augustus Goetz's *The Heiress*, an adaptation
of Henry James's *Washington Square*, directed by John Gielgud at
the Theatre Royal, Haymarket.

There had been stage adaptations of Henry James before but
The Heiress was the first to give James the sort of theatrical success
he had longed for all his life and never achieved. *Washington
Square* describes, with superb irony, the battle which develops
between a commonplace girl and her sardonic father, when she is
courted by an adventurer, who is interested only in her money.

Peggy Ashcroft, in a performance that was infinitely subtle,
acted the original *novella*, as it were, rather than the plodding
adaptation, and turned melodrama into tragedy. The old-
fashioned theatrics, especially on the night when Catherine
waits to elope and Morris Townsend fails to turn up, were
heart-rending. But perhaps even more unforgettable was that
moment, right at the end of the play, when, having dismissed her
lover for good, she is accused of cruelty by her silly aunt. 'Of
course I'm cruel,' she retorts. 'I've been taught by *masters.*'

*Miss Peggy Ashcroft, as Catherine, gives a performance of singular
integrity and power. Setting her face against the temptation to suggest
Cinderella, a poor down-trodden creature who but for neglect might
have blossomed into lovely self-assurance, she presents with almost
clinical precision a study of a girl virtually handicapped by her father's
oppression, who could never, no matter how favourably
circumstanced, have made more than a mediocre impression in the
world. But the fact that this Catherine is a naturally dull girl does not
make her groping after a wider, warmer life any the less affecting, and
Miss Ashcroft moves us deeply.*

Peter Fleming *Spectator*

64 Beatrice in *Much Ado About Nothing* 1950 ▷

The 1950s

65 *Much Ado About Nothing* *1950*

John Gielgud as Benedict, Eric Lander as Claudio, John Wright as Boy, Barbara Jefford as Hero, Mairhi Russell as Margaret, Peggy Ashcroft as Beatrice and Maxine Audley as Ursula in Shakespeare's *Much Ado About Nothing*, directed by John Gielgud at the Memorial Theatre, Stratford-upon-Avon.

John Gielgud's production was one of the rare occasions, these last forty years, when the 'merry war' was fought in its correct Renaissance period, handsomely and theatrically realised by the Italian designer, Mariano Andreu.

Peggy Ashcroft's Beatrice was a charming bluestocking, who dropped bricks all over the place. She and Gielgud's Benedict, affecting a mutually rude indifference, fenced divinely, their skirmishes having an almost Restoration Comedy wit; and this was especially true in their final, ironic acceptance of marriage.

66 *King Lear* *1950*

Peggy Ashcroft as Cordelia and John Gielgud as Lear in Shakespeare's *King Lear*, directed by John Gielgud at the Memorial Theatre, Stratford-upon-Avon.

Such is her impact on the story and in the play itself that it always comes a surprise to realise just how small a role Cordelia is.

Peggy Ashcroft, in a performance of great beauty and touching tenderness, was goodness personified, and the scene in which she is reunited with Lear – her voice ever soft and gentle – was deeply affecting.

I call Peggy Ashcroft's Cordelia perfection. It is impossible for me to imagine the words 'No cause, no cause' more movingly spoken (even, I believe, by Ellen Terry).

Philip Hope-Wallace *Time and Tide*

She has, more than any other actress, the power of touching us simply by her posture and the atmosphere she distils. The change from anxiety to a flooding relief here is beautifully done. Her 'No cause, no cause' is marvellously dropped like two reassuring tears of forgiveness.

T. C. Worsley *New Statesman and Nation*

67 *Twelfth Night* 1950

Alec Clunes as Orsino and Peggy Ashcroft as Viola in Shakespeare's *Twelfth Night*, directed by Hugh Hunt at the Old Vic Theatre.

The first night was a highly emotional occasion, marking, as it did, the reopening of the Old Vic and the return of the Old Vic Company to its home for the first time since the theatre had been bombed in the war in 1941.

Peggy Ashcroft's Viola, subdued and charming, was in welcome contrast to the local inhabitants whose *commedia dell'arte* antics were clearly designed to put Illyria on the tourist map.

To begin with, there is Peggy Ashcroft, the most delightful Viola of my experience. She has passion, she speaks the verse exquisitely, she has her own gift of perennial youth, and she makes a really credible boy. And for the lighter scenes, she has an enchanting gaiety.
W. A. Darlington *Daily Telegraph*

As for Miss Ashcroft, she is as nearly perfect as makes no matter: delicately impassioned, speaking beautifully, and boyish without the slightest trace of mixed hockey.
Eric Keown, *Punch*

68 *Electra* 1951

Peggy Ashcroft as Electra in Sophocles's *Electra*, directed by Michel Saint-Denis at the Old Vic.

The Times did not think Peggy Ashcroft had either the physical or vocal splendour for Greek tragedy, but the real failure of Michel Saint-Denis's production was not with her (far more monumental, in her grief and murderous hate, than Barbara Hepworth's fragile sculpture which shared the same stage, and which would have been more appropriate in a Martha Graham ballet) but rather with the female chorus.

London would have to wait until the 1965 World Theatre season, for a memorable Greek production of Aeschylus's *The Persians*, to see and hear how exciting a Greek chorus could be.

For the part of Electra Miss Ashcroft is built on a small scale, but the scale is often forgotten in the haunting revelation of suffering. Miss Ashcroft can tear the heart out of you with a whisper, and her immense sensibility is matched to the profundity of Electra's grief.
Eric Keown *Punch*

She drives her way through the part with an energy and resolution, and even a hardness which we might have not thought her to possess. She is, no doubt about it, on the grand scale. Her grief is a pure spring gushing from an unquenchionable source: her hate is implacable: her love grows strong as a tree. The assault on our feelings is just about as direct as it could possibly be, striking straight down on us as it should without haze or shadow. In Miss Ashcroft's performance we come as near to experiencing what Greek tragedy should give us as, at this distant date, we can expect.
T. C. Worsley *New Statesman and Nation*

69 *The Merry Wives of Windsor* 1951

Peggy Ashcroft as Mistress Page, Roger Livesey as Falstaff, Brian Smith as Robin and Ursula Jeans as Mistress Ford in Shakespeare's *The Merry Wives of Windsor*, directed by Hugh Hunt at the Old Vic Theatre.

The Merry Wives of Windsor, written in haste to satisfy a royal whim (so tradition has it) is Elizabethan sit com, with Sir John Falstaff, a shadow of his former self, transported from the fifteenth century to Merrie England to become the butt of the bourgeoisie.

Peggy Ashcroft, cast as the more intelligent of these two emancipated wives, entered into the farce with good-humoured vulgarity, and the scene where the fat knight is bundled into the buck-basket, before being thrown into the Thames, was very funny.

70 *The Deep Blue Sea* 1952

Raymond Francis as Jackie Jackson, Kenneth More as Freddie Page and Peggy Ashcroft as Hester Collyer in Terence Rattigan's *The Deep Blue Sea*, directed by Frith Banbury at the Duchess Theatre.

The Deep Blue Sea, once widely thought to be Terence Rattigan's best play, though less likely to last than either *The Winslow Boy* or *The Browning Version*, is about an older woman's obsession for a younger man, who cannot return her love; though anybody, with knowledge of Rattigan's private life, might have guessed that what the story was really about was the obsession of an older man for a younger man.

The play opens with Hester Collyer having just failed to commit suicide. There is a splendid theatrical moment when her lover, an ex-Battle of Britain pilot, unable to come to terms with the post-War years and who spends much of his time pub-crawling, golfing and humiliating his mistress, borrows a shilling to give her to feed the meter – 'Just in case I'm late for dinner'. It

was a role which made Kenneth More's name and he went on playing variations of Freddie for the rest of his acting life.

Peggy Ashcroft scored one of her biggest successes with Hester Collyer, the obsession, sexual frustration and grief, all expertly under-stated.

The grave beauty of Miss Ashcroft's voice, the sad loveliness of her face are unforgettable things; her story of how she fell in love with Freddie Page – and its last words, 'I knew then there was no hope for me – no hope at all' – are almost too heart-rending to be borne.

Harold Hobson *Sunday Times*

Peggy Ashcroft never forces. A dimming of the eye, a barely perceptible catch in the voice, and an audience is at her feet. No one can so move with sorrow-in-stillness.

J. C. Trewin *Illustrated London News*

71 *The Merchant of Venice*
1953

Robert Shaw as Gratiano, Michael
Redgrave as Shylock, Philip Morant as the
Duke of Venice, Peggy Ashcroft as Portia,
Marigold Charlesworth as Nerissa,
Michael Turner as Solanio, Harry
Andrews as Antonio, David King as the
goaler, Tony Britton as Bassanio and
William Peacock as Salerio in
Shakespeare's *The Merchant of Venice*,
directed by Denis Carey at the Memorial
Theatre, Stratford-upon-Avon.

73 *Antony and Cleopatra* 1953

Michael Redgrave as Antony and Peggy Ashcroft as Cleopatra in Shakespeare's *Antony and Cleopatra*, directed by Glen Byam Shaw at the Memorial Theatre, Stratford-upon-Avon. The production transferred to the Princes Theatre.

Cleopatra is a lady of such infinite variety, her moods changing, not only scene by scene, but often line by line, that it is rare for an actress to be able to encompass the whole role.

Many people, feeling that Peggy Ashcroft was physically and temperamentally all wrong, could not see how she could possibly succeed. Queen, yes. Majestic rhetoric, yes. Gaudy nights, no. Whore, certainly not. In the event, though she inevitably divided the critics, she succeeded beyond most critics' expectations.

Pale-faced and red-wigged, she was certainly no Egyptian dish, but rather a wily Greek, whose cunning, wit, sadism and passion were all vividly there.

Cleopatra, as seen through the biased eyes of Rome (despite Octavius's unexpected glowing tribute) might seem too vulgar for tragedy, and certainly her death scene is as rich and sumptuous a spectacle as anything she has stage-managed before, though, possibly, in slightly better taste. Peggy Ashcroft, no gypsy, made the royal leave-taking unmistakably tragic.

We are so used to seeing her in domestic affliction and the tranquilities of homespun tragedy that her power to show tyrannical caprice and loose-mouthed lickerish dominion over her Antony is the more remarkable. That she should triumph in the poetry of Cleopatra was a natural guess; that she would so rise to the display of spite, rage and bliss in fevered fury one did not surmise.

Ivor Brown *Observer*

There is nothing she cannot express by her exquisite acting, except emotion on a large scale; as a result her Cleopatra is beautifully conceived but in a small focus. Set beside Mr Redgrave's bigger and lustier portrait it becomes a miniature of fine workmanship, containing all the essence of Cleopatra but missing the element of tempest.

Eric Keown *Punch*

The summing up must be that Miss Ashcroft touched with silver a part which needs burnishing with gold. We must record a failure but a gallant one in good company.

Kenneth Tynan *Evening Standard*

The point about her is that, in spite of her natural disadvantages, she achieves the role; and, having waited twenty-five years to see that done, I am at her feet. Her success has the additional spice of being a triumph over general expectation.

T. C. Worsley *New Statesman and Nation*

72 *The Merchant of Venice* 1953

Peggy Ashcroft as Portia in Shakespeare's *The Merchant of Venice*.

There were those – perhaps because she was acting in a different key to Michael Redgrave's ferocious Shylock – who thought Peggy Ashcroft was lacking both in high spirits and hardness; but for most critics, the quiet wit and very stillness was her great strength, giving the casket and trial scenes, a genuine rather than a theatrical feeling.

74 *Antony and Cleopatra*   *1953*

Robert Shaw as Dolabella, Peggy Ashcroft
as Cleopatra and Marius Goring as
Octavius Caesar in Shakespeare's *Antony
and Cleopatra*.

75 *Hedda Gabler* 1954

Peggy Ashcroft as Hedda, George Devine as Tesman and Alan Badel as Lovborg in Henrik Ibsen's *Hedda Gabler*, directed by Peter Ashmore at the Lyric Theatre, Hammersmith. The production transferred to the Westminster Theatre.

An audience, arriving at the theatre, expecting to see a tragedy and Ibsenite gloom, found instead a brilliant high comedy; but then Hedda – as Max Beerbohm had observed, in 1903, having seen Eleonora Duse in the role – ought to be played with a sense of humour.

Peggy Ashcroft's Hedda's sense of humour was always lethal in its irony, whether she was offending Miss Tesman over her new bonnet, terrifying poor Thea by threatening to burn her hair, mocking her husband behind his back and to his face, or sparring with Judge Brack. She was a totally unsympathetic and calculatingly evil character.

This Hedda, socially and sexually frustrated, constantly shivering as if unable ever to get warm, had danced herself to a standstill, and was bored. It was the aching boredom Peggy Ashcroft emphasised most.

The production later toured Scandinavia and, in Oslo, King Haakon of Norway awarded her the King's Gold Medal.

It is curious to have to register that an English actress has shown the Norwegian public how Hedda should be played.

Aftenposten Norway

76 *Hedda Gabler* 1954

George Devine as Tesman, Michael MacLiammoir as Brack and Peggy Ashcroft as Hedda in Henrik Ibsen's *Hedda Gabler*.

This performance is the most impressive piece of individual acting I can recall during the post-War years.

W. A. Darlington *Daily Telegraph*

The purple-patched part of Hedda is the dramatic actress's dream, and last night Miss Peggy Ashcroft realised it with a brilliance I have not seen equalled.

J. P. W. Mallalieu, MP *Evening Standard*

In future I shall set no limits on this actress's dramatic powers.

Cecil Wilson *Daily Mail*

She gave a performance that will be talked about by theatregoers for a decade.

Paul Holt *Herald*

77 *Much Ado About Nothing* 1955

John Gielgud as Benedict and Peggy Ashcroft as Beatrice in Shakespeare's *Much Ado About Nothing*, directed by John Gielgud at the Palace Theatre.

John Gielgud's classic and much-loved production, which had been playing off and on for the last six years, returned to London, following a long tour abroad.

Miss Ashcroft has no equal in this country for that rare combination of featherweight touch and attack; her high spirits are the most infectious thing in the world, and never for an instant do we sense their assumption by a skillful actress.

J. W. Lambert *Sunday Times*

Miss Ashcroft is an enchanting Beatrice; she still affects a fluttering movement in pretty evocation of the 'lapwing' lines, still gives the raillery and 'divine discourse' a lovely mixture of wit, gaiety and passion. And even if her manner carries a tinge of decorum where one might expect a nettlesome Rennaissance attack she takes the part with great elegance and spirit.

Derek Granger *Financial Times*

78 *The Chalk Garden* 1956

Mavis Walker as the Nurse, Peggy Ashcroft as Miss Madrigal and Edith Evans as Mrs St Maugham in Enid Bagnold's *The Chalk Garden*, directed by John Gielgud at the Theatre Royal, Haymarket.

Miss Madrigal is a governess, without references, having just spent fifteen years in jail as a reprieved murderer. There was a good, if very contrived moment when she asks the judge, who has been invited to lunch, and who just happened to have presided at her trial, if he is going to tell her employer who she is, only to find, that until that instant, he had not recognised her.

Peggy Ashcroft, as awkward in her movements as in her speech, movingly suggested that Miss Madrigal, as much as the young girl in her charge, was in need of care and attention. Sitting tensely on the edge of her chair, the very tightness of the grip on herself, conveying a bundle of nerves, she rivetted attention, and never more so than when she was saying nothing.

'Did you do it?' asks her employer, the worldly Mrs St Maugham with all Edith Evans's familiar voice-swooping *grande dame* aplomb. It was the contrast between the two actresses, the witty artificiality of the one and the genuine reality of the other, which gave the play an extra dimension.

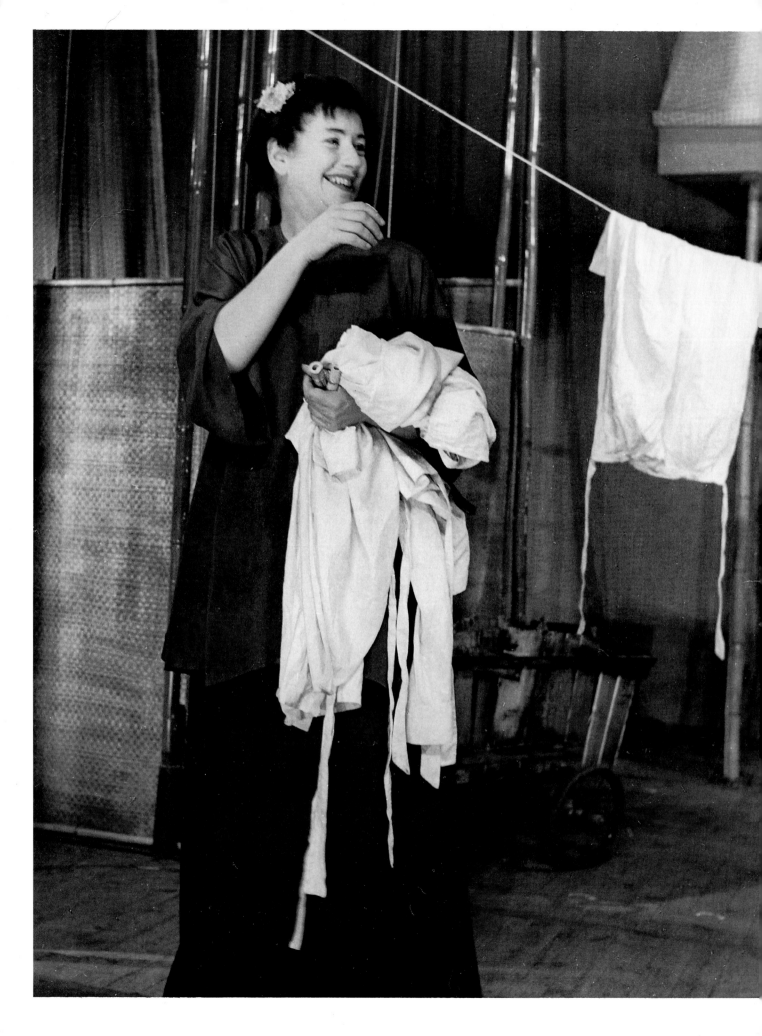

79 The Good Woman of Setzuan 1956

Peggy Ashcroft as Shen Te in Bertolt Brecht's *The Good Woman of Setzuan*, directed by George Devine, for the English Stage Company at the Royal Court Theatre.

This Marxist parable, about the difficulties of being good in a wicked world, was the first full-scale production of a Brecht play in English, and arrived in the wake of the Berliner Ensemble's memorable visit to London, in a season which had included *Mother Courage*, with Helen Weigel. The Brechtian style initially proved a bit elusive and the Berliner Ensemble would have to come back with an equally memorable production of *The Threepenny Opera*, with Wolf Kaiser as Mack the Knife, before British directors and actors would begin to get Brecht right.

Peggy Ashcroft played the good woman, a prostitute turned tobacconist who, realising that her kindness and generosity will be her financial ruin, invents a ruthless male cousin to protect her business interests, and then finds she has to produce him. She impersonates him herself.

The two roles allowed for a virtuoso transformation. There were those, like Kenneth Tynan, who thought her prostitute smacked too much of Kensington and were more convinced by her male entrepreneur.

The scene in which Shen Te tells the story of the cranes, to prevent a pilot from committing suicide, was one of the most touching in the play.

80 The Good Woman of Setzuan 1956

Peggy Ashcroft as Shui Ta in Bertolt Brecht's *The Good Woman of Setzuan*.

Shui Ta was the male cousin: a half-masked, felt-hatted, cheroot-smoking, shoulder-rolling spiv.

Nothing tougher has been heard since Montgomery last harangued the troops.

Kenneth Tynan *Evening Standard*

81 As You Like It 1957

Richard Johnson as Orlando, Peggy Ashcroft as Rosalind, Doreen Aris as Phebe and Robert Arnold as Silvius in Shakespeare's *As You Like It*, directed by Glen Byam Shaw at the Memorial Theatre, Stratford-upon-Avon.

When I wonder, is Dame Peggy going to lose that miraculous gift of youth? Probably never. Once can see her like Ellen Terry continuing to deny rather than defy the years until she is an old lady. Even now she makes nonsense of arithmetic. Who could believe, to see her boyish bearing in the part tonight that she had been old enough to play Rosalind twenty-odd years ago?

W. A. Darlington *Daily Telegraph*

82 *Cymbeline* 1957

Peggy Ashcroft as Imogen in Shakespeare's *Cymbeline*, directed by Peter Hall at the Memorial Theatre, Stratford-upon-Avon.

The nineteenth century tended to idealise Imogen; Alfred, Lord Tennyson even went so far as to arrange for a copy of *Cymbeline* to be buried with him. Today the play is out of favour, and rarely disintered.

Peter Hall's production was a pretty Grimm fairy tale in which the full horror of Imogen, waking to find, by her side, a headless man, whom she takes to be her husband, was, perhaps, not fully appreciated.

Mr Hall has in Peggy Ashcroft an Imogen who, being sad and vulnerable herself, is at odds with the superficial extravagancies and gaieties of the production. The result is that Dame Peggy's most tragic moments come into headlong collision with Mr Hall's imaginative burlesque. When this magnificent actress, in that rich voice which can express all pain in its compass, cries out, 'O Posthumus, where is thy head?' it is a melancholy thing to hear the theatre swept by a gale of delighted merriment.

Harold Hobson *Sunday Times*

83 *The Nun's Story* 1958

Audrey Hepburn as Sister Luke and Peggy Ashcroft as Mother Mathilde in the film version of Kathryn C. Hulme's *The Nun's Story*, directed by Fred Zinnemann.

Sister Luke, a member of a Belgian order of nursing nuns, finally has to admit what she already knows – that she has no vacation for convent life.

Peggy Ashcroft played the Reverend Mother who was responsible for her during her stay in the Congo.

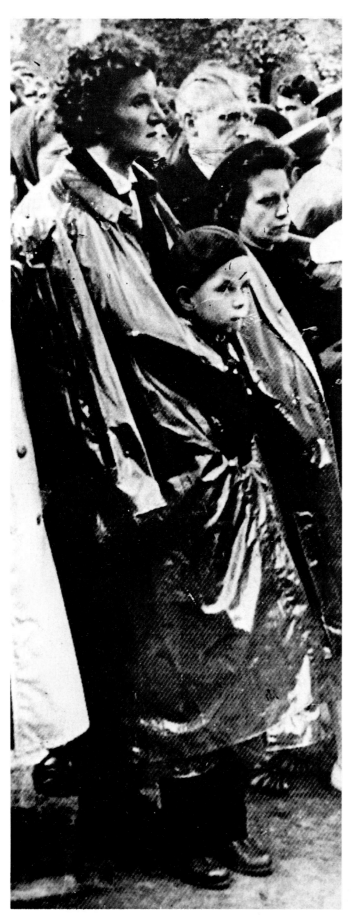

85 *Shadow of Heroes* 1958

Peggy Ashcroft as Julia Rajk and John Pike as the young Lazlo Rajk in Robert Ardrey's *Shadow of Heroes*, directed by Peter Hall at the Piccadilly Theatre.

Shadow of Heroes, a semi-documentary drama about the 1956 Hungarian Uprising, gained enormously from its immediacy, the audience arriving at the theatre, still vividly remembering the cries for help which had come over the radio and been ignored by the world.

Julia Rajk was the wife of the Hungarian communist leader, who had been executed by his own party. The most moving moment was when Emlyn Williams, speaking for the author, said that nothing had been heard of her since the uprising, that she had not authorised the play, but that they didn't think, it could, in any way, worsen her present condition.

Peggy Ashcroft (looking extraordinarily like Julia Rajk) characteristically underplayed the speech at the Petofi Club, in Budapest, which had been in part responsible for the uprising, almost throwing it away.

84 The photograph on the left is a picture of Julia Rajk and her son, Lazlo, taken in Hungary, at the time these events were taking place.

86 Rosmersholm 1959

Mark Dignam as Mr Kroll, Peggy Ashcroft as Rebecca West and Eric Porter as John Rosmer in Henrik Ibsen's *Rosmersholm*, directed by George Devine, for the English Stage Company, at the Royal Court Theatre. The production transferred to the Comedy Theatre in 1960.

Rosmersholm, intellectually and emotionally, never the easiest of plays to perform, preaches a broader, freer, more open-minded attitude to sex and politics; but Rebecca West and John Rosmer, products of the nineteenth century, are not nearly so emancipated as either they or we had been led to believe; and the truth about their relationship, so long suppressed, kills them.

Peggy Ashcroft, true to what Ibsen had wanted, underplayed, denying some audiences the melodrama they might have preferred, especially in the difficult last act, which is almost Greek Tragedy and Grand Opera rolled into one. However, this did not mean that the heavy burden of guilt (Rebecca had slept

with her father and driven Rosmer's first wife to suicide) was any the less appalling or that the passion was any the less wild for being acted naturalistically; and besides, Peggy Ashcroft was always, in little ways, suggesting that Rebecca's 'calm resolution' might break at any minute.

Peggy Ashcroft's performance as Rebecca also has its minority of bitter critics. Her mannerisms often seem to be manipulating her – the lips become paralysed in that moue which women make when they are putting on lipstick, the voice goes rippling and foaming over the sibilants while the mind is lagging behind, and she has the general air of a highly strung schoolmistress about to throw a fit of the vapours. But these seem to me to fit this part like a glove – they are the mannerisms of a real individual, not just the gimmicks of a personality saleswoman.

Alan Brien *Spectator*

87 Duchess in *The Duchess of Malfi* 1960 ▷

The 1960s

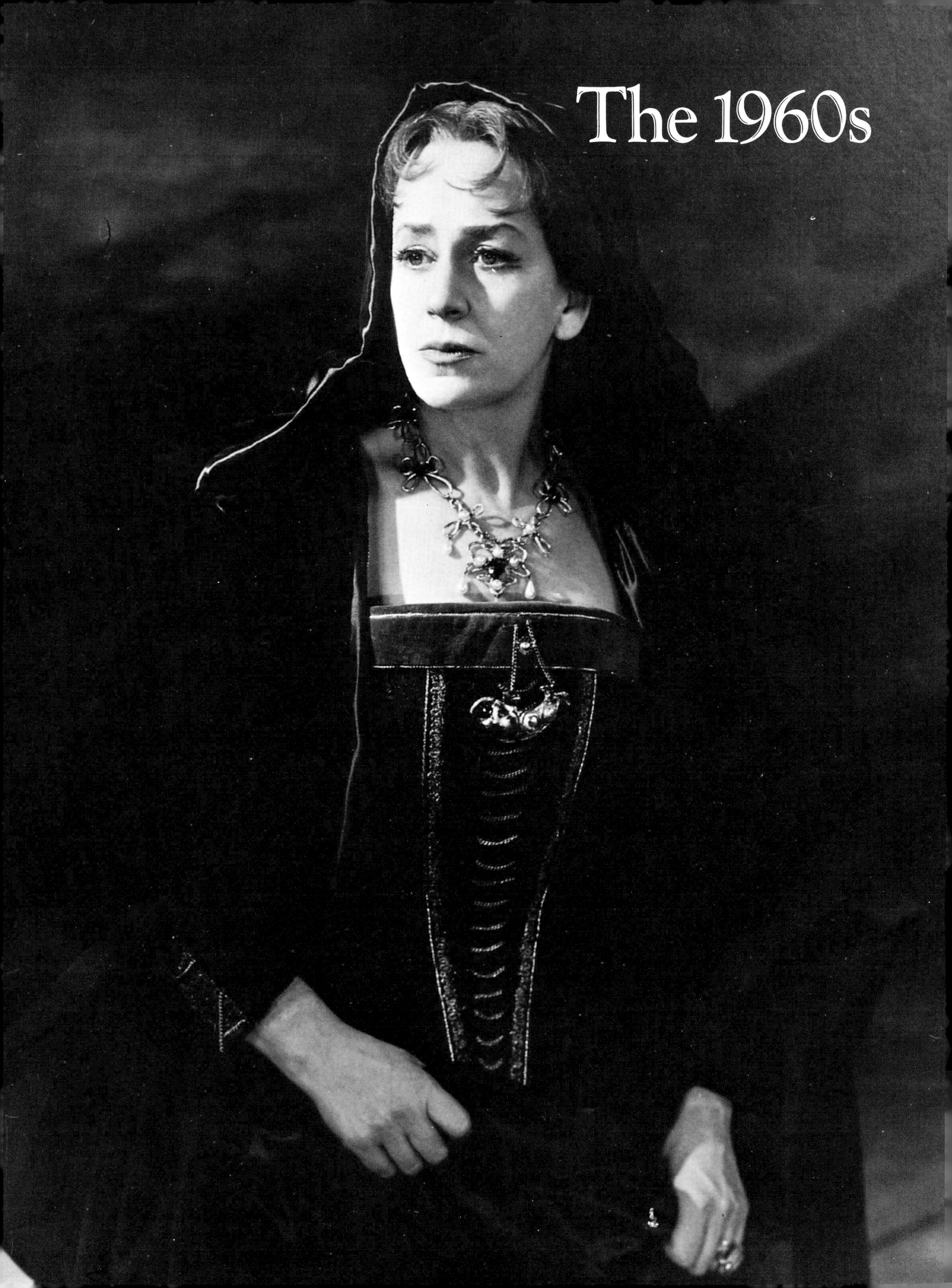

88 The Taming of the Shrew   1960

Peggy Ashcroft as Katharina and Peter O'Toole as Petruchio in
Shakespeare's *The Taming of the Shrew*, directed by John Barton
at the Memorial Theatre, Stratford-upon-Avon.

It is not unusual nowadays to act *The Taming of the Shrew* for
comedy (Charles Marowitz once directed it as if it were *The
Duchess of Malfi*), but, in 1960, there was general surprise at
finding there was more to the play than mere knockabout farce.

Many people thought Katharina would be totally alien to
Peggy Ashcroft's temperament, and quite outside her range as an
actress. What she did, and it is perhaps the only way to make the
text more acceptable to a modern audience, was to have
Katharina fall in love with Petruchio right from the start. The
role gained enormously in humour and pathos.

The re-thinking of the play was continued when the
production was revived the following year with Vanessa
Redgrave.

*Peggy Ashcroft, in prospect an impossible Kate, confounds prophecy
by demonstrating herself ideal for the part; it was her predecessors who
were impossible. This is no striding virago, no Lady Macbeth
manquée, instead, we have a sulky girl who has developed into a school
bully and a family scold to spite her sister, Bianca.*
                                    Kenneth Tynan *Observer*

*In such a strident part it is incredible that a great actress could actually
increase her reputation. But this is the miracle that Dame Peggy
performs. From her first entrance there is a radiance hidden behind
Katharina's sullenness, waiting to be released, and at the end Dame
Peggy is a woman liberated, not a woman cowed.*
                                    Harold Hobson *Sunday Times*

89 The Winter's Tale   1960

Peggy Ashcroft as Paulina in Shakespeare's *The Winter's Tale*,
directed by Peter Wood at the Memorial Theatre, Stratford-
upon-Avon.

Paulina is best remembered for her tongue: a woman loud in
her integrity and even louder in her indignation. Peggy
Ashcroft's originality was to cut down on the steam-rolling
termagency, with the result that Paulina came across as a much
nicer person than usual; and though there were those who would
have preferred something a bit more robust, the part lost none of
its authority.

The other surprise, such is its rarity, was not that Hermione,
on her pedestal, had kept her youth but that, sixteen years later,
Paulina had visibly aged. It gave the final scenes an additional
pathos.

90 *The Duchess of Malfi* *1960*

Max Adrian as the Cardinal, Eric Porter as Ferdinand and Peggy Ashcroft as the Duchess in John Webster's *The Duchess of Malfi*, directed by Donald McWhinnie at the Aldwych Theatre.

The Stratford-upon-Avon Company opened their first London season with this production, the play's first revival since 1945. Peggy Ashcroft, returning to Webster's dark chamber of horrors, for a second time, was magnificent in the scene which led up to her strangulation, giving the Duchess unmistakable majesty in adversity:

> *What would it pleasure me to have my throat cut*
> *With diamonds? or to be smothered*
> *With cassia? or to be shot to death with pearls?*
> *I know death has ten thousand doors*
> *For men to take their exits;*

If the terrible sufferings of the heroine are to be represented in the grand manner, Dame Peggy Ashcroft is vocally inadequate and physically she cannot quite fill the romantic mind's eye. But her miniature of the Duchess not only glows with colour and character and vitality but it is painted with great power. The scene of her stooping to conquer her steward is alive with vivacity and sincerity, and she faces her tortures with moving fortitude and dignity.

The Times

91 *Othello* *1961*

Peggy Ashcroft as Emelia and Dorothy Tutin as Desdemona in Shakespeare's *Othello*, directed by Franco Zeffirelli at the Royal Shakespeare Theatre, Stratford-upon-Avon.

Zeffirelli's production, with John Gielgud as the Moor, had a first night which is unlikely to be forgotten by either the actors or the audience. Everything went wrong: the scene changes were interminable, pillars wobbled, beards came off, lines were forgotten, and Iago declared that Cassio was dead.

Peggy Ashcroft, a somewhat ladylike Emelia, was at her best, in the *Willow Song* scene, with Dorothy Tutin.

1961

The first time I met and worked with Peggy was during The Cherry Orchard when she gave me enormous help through a difficult rehearsal period. It is one of the qualities I admire in her that she should take so much care of young people in the profession.

She possesses great courage and great strength. She is quite fearless in her opinions. Both on-stage and off-stage, she never takes the easy way out. She constantly surprises. How typical that when she accepted the award for best actress in A Passage to India, she should express her delight in sharing the same platform as Bob Geldorf! No wonder she is so loved by the profession and the public.

My own affection and admiration for Peggy is very great indeed.

Judi Dench

92 *The Cherry Orchard* 1961

George Murcell as Lopahin, Paul Hardwick as Pishchik, Patience Collier as Charlotta, Roy Dotrice as Firs, Dorothy Tutin as Varya, Peggy Ashcroft as Mme Ranevsky, John Gielgud as Gaev, Patsy Byrne as Dunyasha and Judi Dench as Anya in Anton Chekhov's *The Cherry Orchard*, directed by Michel Saint-Denis, for the Royal Shakespeare Company, at the Aldwych Theatre.

The cherry orchard is Ranevsky's life, her youth, her happiness, her Russia. The whole of the third act, when she does not know what has happened at the auction, and her dismay and collapse, when she learns it is *Lopahin*, who has bought the orchard, was beautifully played.

So, too, was that scene, in the second act, when she is talking about her lover in Paris, at once absurd yet poignant, catching all the charm and weakness of this self-indulgent, frivolous, scatterbrained, maddening woman.

93 *The Wars of the Roses*   1963

David Warner as Henry VI and Peggy Ashcroft as Margaret of
Anjou in Shakespeare's *The Wars of the Roses*, directed by Peter
Hall, for the Royal Shakespeare Company, at the Royal
Shakespeare Theatre, Stratford-upon-Avon.

The Wars of the Roses, a landmark in the Royal Shakespeare
Company's achievements, and one of the most exciting and
rewarding theatrical experiences of the 1960s, was the three parts
of *Henry VI*, freely adapted to make two plays, plus *Richard III*.

Margaret of Anjou, She-Wolf of France, Cassandra-like in her
cursing, and the Terror of the House of York, personifies all the
bitter hatred and carnage of the Civil War. It is a Sarah Siddons
of a role, as physically taxing and technically demanding as
anything Peggy Ashcroft had ever done, requiring the greatest
stamina and resources, especially on those Saturdays when the
whole cycle was performed in one day, starting at ten-thirty in
the morning and not finishing until gone eleven at night.

One of the advantages of being able to see Margaret in the
Henry VI plays first was that an audience, by the time they got to
Richard III, knew why and what she was raving on about, in a way
they had rarely, if ever, done in the past.

Peggy Ashcroft held the trilogy together, sustaining the
rhetoric, and developed from an eighteen-year-old wanton to a

crazy old witch, every ugly facet of her character, brutally and
pitifully revealed; and never more so than when, triumphing over
the captured Duke of York, she wiped his face with a napkin,
dipped in his son's blood: 'I pr'ythee grieve to make me merry.'

The performance was unforgettable in its savage humour, its
hysterical laughter and tears, its eloquence, its intensity, and,
finally, in its physical deformity.

94 *The Wars of the Roses*   1963

Hugh Sullivan as Lord Hastings, Peggy Ashcroft as Queen
Margaret, Jeffery Dench as the Earl of Derby, Ian Holm as
Richard, Duke of Gloucester, and Tom Fleming as the Duke of
Buckingham in Shakespeare's *The Wars of the Roses*.

---

*What first attracted me to the idea of playing the part? The problem of
presenting with credibility a woman who could carry her lover's severed
head on to the stage and play a scene holding it in her arms.*

Peggy Ashcroft

95 *The Seagull* 1964

Peggy Ashcroft as Mme Arkadina and Peter Finch as Trigorin in Anton Chekhov's *The Seagull*, directed by George Devine, for the English Stage Company, at the Queen's Theatre.

The idea that Peggy Ashcroft might be miscast, not being thought actressy enough, was squashed on her first entrance, when she immediately established not only Arkadina's boredom and insensitivity but her vulgarity as well.

The third act, when she begs Trigorin to stay, throwing herself at his feet, degradingly piling superlative on superlative, until he has no option but to stay, came across with its full comic irony. It was almost as if Arkadina were acting in one of those tatty plays with which she used to tour the provinces. A classic case of Life imitating Art.

Peggy Ashcroft chooses to emphasise in Madame Arkadina the ageing beauty rather than the provincial actress. Her monopoly of the limelight is not achieved imperiously; it is done with pouts, with coy wheedles of the voice, with a fidgeting of her bare shoulders when she is forced to watch Nina in Konstantin's play. Her boast that she could still play a fifteen-year-old girl is reinforced by the fact that she spends most of her time doing so.

Bamber Gascoigne *Observer*

The keen brilliance and eagerness of Peggy Ashcroft do not serve the role, as I see it. Needless to say, and nervous tremulous mannerisms apart, this was a striking assumption of the part; but it seemed petulant where it needed to be egocentrically voluptuous.

Philip Hope-Wallace *Guardian*

96 *Days in the Trees* 1966

Peggy Ashcroft as the mother and George Baker as her son in Marguerite Duras's *Days in the Trees*, directed by John Schlesinger, for the Royal Shakespeare Company, at the Aldwych Theatre.

A rich old lady, who runs a thriving factory in a remote French colony, comes home to indulge her gigolo son, whom she admires and loves with a passionate affection, which is only matched by her passionate contempt for all those ugly imbeciles who *work* for a living.

Days in the Trees was a bit boring on both a realistic and symbolic level, but Peggy Ashcroft, in a role notable for its gargantuan appetite and garrulity, was technically highly accomplished. Her performance, almost birdlike in her voice and movements, saved the day; though Harold Hobson, a champion of Marguerite Duras's work in England, complained, in the *Sunday Times*, that she had entirely reversed the play's political meaning.

The production was seen on television the following year.

Dame Peggy's performance as the barmy old bitch will take a terrible beating when we sit down to tot up the score for the best acting of the year.

Maurice Wiggin *Sunday Times*

97 Ghosts 1967

John Castle as Oswald and Peggy Ashcroft as Mrs Alving in Henrik Ibsen's *Ghosts*, directed by Alan Bridges, for the Royal Shakespeare Company, at the Aldwych Theatre.

It is so rare for modern revivals of *Ghosts* to live up to the original London reviews ('the most loathesome play ever put upon the stage . . . an open drain . . . morbid, unhealthy, unwholesome, disgusting . . . garbage and offal') that often it is more exciting to stay at home and read the *Daily Telegraph* editorial, for 14 March 1891, in full.

Ibsen dared to write about things which many people, at the time, felt were best left unsaid. *Ghosts* is like a jigsaw puzzle, which an audience gradually pieces together to reveal, when all the lies and hypocrisy have been stripped away, a syphilitic truth.

Peggy Ashcroft, pale and haunted, subtly conveyed the personal cost to Mrs Alving of having kept the knowledge from her son for so long, but the big emotional scene between them, leading to the fatal dose of morphine, was less than harrowing.

In most productions of the play, it is difficult to imagine that there could ever have been anything between Mrs Alving and Pastor Manders. What Peggy Ashcroft did was to convey she *still* had an affection for him, and it made the remembrance, of the night she had rejected her, touching in a way it had not been before.

98 *From Chekhov With Love* 1968

Peggy Ashcroft as Olga Knipper, Maurice Denham as Alexander
Chekhov, John Gielgud as Anton Chekhov, Dorothy Tutin as
Maria, Nigel Davenport as Maxim Gorky and Wendy Hiller as
Mme Avilova in *From Chekhov With Love*, staged by Jonathan
Miller and directed by Bill Turner for Rediffusion Television.

From Chekhov With Love was a portrait of the Russian
playwright's life built up through letters from and to him. The
production was a series of stylised tableaux.

Olga Knipper, a founder member of the Moscow Arts Theatre,
married Chekhov in 1901. She created Mme Arkadina in *The
Seagull* and Mme Ranevsky in *The Cherry Orchard* – two roles
Peggy Ashcroft herself would play some sixty years later.

99 *Secret Ceremony* 1968

Peggy Ashcroft and Pamela Brown in *Secret Ceremony*, a film directed by Joseph Losey.

Secret Ceremony starred Elizabeth Taylor as an ageing prostitute and Mia Farrow as a strange young girl, who uses her as a substitute mother. This schizophrenic melodrama was chiefly praised, at the time, for the baroque extravagance of its setting, a fantastic mansion.

Peggy Ashcroft and Pamela Brown played two dotty aunts, Pinteresque scavengers, on the look-out for knick-knacks for their antique shop.

100 *Three Into Two Won't Go* 1969

Claire Bloom, Rod Steiger and Peggy Ashcroft in *Three Into Two Won't Go*, a film directed by Peter Hall.

Rod Steiger played an unhappily married salesmanager, who has an affair with a nineteen-year-old hitch-hiker, who turns up at his house, claiming she is pregnant. Claire Bloom played his childless wife.

Peggy Ashcroft was cast as his slightly unhinged mother-in-law, a lonely widow, who has been dumped in an old people's home. She, too, in her time, had been a deceived wife and had had to learn to live with it, and quite obviously never had.

101 A Delicate Balance 1969

Elizabeth Spriggs as Claire, Sheila Hancock as Julia, Peggy Ashcroft as Agnes and Michael Hordern as Tobias in Edward Albee's *A Delicate Balance*, directed by Peter Hall, for the Royal Shakespeare Company, at the Aldwych Theatre.

Agnes, long embittered by the loss of her child and her husband's unfaithfulness, is the fulcrum upon which her family is supported. It is a balancing act she resents, and which is disturbed by the arrival of two unwanted guests who, just when the audience has accepted them as symbols, disconcertingly turn out to be real people.

Peggy Ashcroft matched Agnes's glacial wit and stoicism with icy composure and cultivated detachment; it was a highly articulate and extremely elegant performance with two fine speeches – one on the plague the visitors have brought and the other, an invocation to the dawn.

But what stays in the memory, long after Albee's drawingroom metaphysics have been forgotten, is the story Agnes's husband tells of killing his cat when it suddenly and inexplicably ceased to love him.

102 Landscape 1969

David Waller as Duff and Peggy Ashcroft as Beth in Harold
Pinter's *Landscape*, directed by Peter Hall, for the Royal
Shakespeare Company, at the Aldwych Theatre.

A husband and wife, chauffeur and housekeeper, sit apart in
the kitchen of an empty country house, never moving from their
chairs, the rift between them emphasised by a fissure in John
Bury's set.

Landscape, first performed on radio, is a play for two voices:
one, coarse and brutal; the other, quiet and gentle. The two
parallel monologues make, with their all-important pauses and
silences, one continuous piece of music.

The chauffeur does all the talking. The housekeeper is so
immersed in her memory of making love on a deserted beach
years before that, not only does she not hear him, she does not
even seem to be aware he is talking, so successfully does she shut
him out.

Giving equal weight to what was said and left unsaid, Peggy
Ashcroft acted Pinter's threnodic mosaic with consummate
technical skill. In remembering one moment of happiness (with a
man, who might have been her employer or, even possibly, her
husband) she suggested a lifetime's loneliness. It was a
performance of great simplicity and lyrical tenderness, the last six
lines, ending with 'Oh my true love I said,' being particularly
moving.

Four years later, when *Landscape* was revived in a double-bill,
with Pinter's *A Slight Ache*, she would bring Beth fractionally
down the social ladder, without losing any of the poetry.

I shall never forget her performance in my play Landscape. *Frozen
forever in memories of lost or imagined love, she sat in the willed prison
of her kitchen chair, at one and the same time griefstricken and radiant.
A miraculous synthesis. A wonderful actress.*

Harold Pinter

103 Henry VIII 1969

Donald Sinden as Henry and Peggy Ashcroft as Katherine of
Aragon in Shakespeare's *Henry VIII*, directed by Trevor Nunn,
for the Royal Shakespeare Company, at the Royal Shakespeare
Theatre, Stratford-upon-Avon. The production transferred to
the Aldwych Theatre.

Henry VIII is a boring history play few people want to see
twice. The only possible way to do it is with the sort of spectacle
the Victorian and Edwardian theatre-goer used to enjoy. In this
revival, there was one magical moment right at the very end
when Archbishop Cranmer's patriotic speech developed into a
prayer, by the whole company, for 'peace, plenty, love and
truth'.

Peggy Ashcroft's Queen, very subdued, beautifully spoken,
began with all the authority of a Holbein portrait, and ended
looking like a frail old lady as painted by Rembrandt. Her trial
scene might have been even more poignant if the King had not
thought he was acting in Alexander Korda's tongue-in-cheek
screen version, *The Private Life of Henry VIII*.

Memoirs, and pen portraits, are often more revealing of the writer than the subject, and equally often leave that subject in bewildered discomfort, unable to recognize the character emerging from the anecdotes. So I am confident that Dame Peggy Ashcroft will both chortle and frown; her instinct is to be generous, but I will assumedly be told frankly and firmly if she feels that she has been misrepresented.

Peggy won't remember anything at all about the first time we were in the same room, even though the room was only eight feet square. It was immediately behind the stage door keeper's kiosk at the Aldwych Theatre and it boasted the only television set in the building. It was six o'clock on a Monday evening. I had joined the Royal Shakespeare Company, as an assistant director only a few months previously, and England were playing Australia in the Test Series. I had taken to watching the end of each day's play in the snuggery of that most talkative afficciando, Cliff, the doorman. As I sat down in the tiny darkened room, illuminated only by the flickering of Cliff's black and white set, I realised that there was somebody else there, somebody who was very emotionally aroused by England's inability to break through the Australian tail.

'Damn . . . Oh, nooo . . . Hell . . .'

At 6.30, as E. W. Swanton started his round up, the light in the room was switched on and who I had thought must be a noisy boy turned out to be one of the great ladies of the English stage, in a brown trouser suit and a brown study.

'Hopeless,' she said to Cliff, who was agreeing with her that the ashes looked well and truly lost again.

Ad she disappeared with her dressing room key, I mouthed the name 'Peggy Ashcroft?' to Cliff.

'Oh, yes, that was the Dame,' he said. 'Cricket crazy.'

I once spent a day at Lords with Peggy and we watched a sturdy young English Yeoman called John Hampshire stride out and hit a maiden test century against Gary Sobers' West Indies. We agreed that more than all other games, cricket could induce national pride. As Hampshire passed the 100 mark, we were joyous and brimful of tears.

'Ah, that's real theatre,' said Peg.

Peggy has a very clear sense of when things aren't cricket. She believes in 'the team', in the importance of every member of the team and believes, to a rare and childlike extent, in playing fair. She is utterly loyal to friends and family and she can be extremely partisan, but her loyalties never dissuade her from being honest or demanding honesty.

I suspect because of her sense of permanence and family, she never actively pursued the available avenues of commercial stardom in either the theatre or the cinema. She only allows herself to become involved with what is genuinely demanding and she needs to work in the company of people who all feel that the play is more important than its component parts.

Against this, possibly unsuspected background, she is inspirational. The greatest actors do not disguise themselves, they reveal themselves; the greatness in the actor must proceed somehow from greatness in the person.

Peggy has played many parts in the knowledge that they have been played superbly by others in generations before. It takes a very special largesse and generosity not to resent the achievements of your predecessors as you embark on your own account of a classic role, but trusting your own responses to an infinitely complex part, like Cleopatra, amounts to trusting the workings of your innermost self. Trust is often another word for risk. Peggy does both, not without fears and tears, but expressing an instinct that in every sense she must put herself on the line.

This leads Peggy to identify with her roles to the point where the vision of actress and character are indivisible. When we did Henry VIII together, in which she played Katherine of Aragon (for which she won the Evening Standard Award), Peggy spent weeks feeling a vague but disquieting sense of injustice. Eventually she came to me and said that there were important arguments missing from her trial defense. She provided me with several extra lines, which either accused Henry or further exonerated Katharine.

'But, Peg,' I said. 'We're doing a play by Shakespeare, not a documentary on Katherine.'

'Yes, but Shakespeare doesn't let me defend myself properly. It's a conspiracy against me to let Henry off the hook . . .'

The lines never went in, but the pain of the injustice informed every moment of her Katherine's lingering existence.

Peggy carries with her much suffering for unpunished injustice. Her causes are many and various; radical, intolerant of cant and cover-up, incapable of inaction, she has marched, protested and demonstrated, written her disagreements with governments and policies, and given her time, talent and money in countless charitable causes to make a better world. Having shared a house with Peggy, I have heard her talk on a lot of issues, political, racial and moral. She is a Utopian; and I, for one, would be happy to live in the world she describes.

Her Utopia is born of the slings and arrows, of a lifetime of involvement, there is no escapism from the realities, but it is also informed by a child's vision of happiness. Peggy can startle a company of younger actors with her girlishness, her shrieks, her laughter, her sheer physical energy in the grip of a role. I confess I think of her no differently from the day when I first met her, though twenty years have passed.

Our first proper contact did not bode well. She was appearing in a production of Ibsen's Ghosts at the Aldwych Theatre. The show had become unfocussed, the director was elsewhere, and Peter Hall instructed me (as an RSC assistant) to take some rehearsals.

I was excited and nervous. I called the company for 10.30 the following morning. A message from the Dame urged me to make the call a bit later. I stuck to my guns – 10.30 it was. Then I fell victim to a freakish series of events. My alarm clock stopped dead in the middle of the night and my belt and braces telephone alarm call never came through since my telephone had also gone out of order. The stage management, waiting with a full company in the rehearsal room, were unable to contact me.

Eventually, I was woken by a hammering on the door from a search party at twelve o'clock, and oddly dressed and in tumult I arrived at the rehearsal room off Leicester Square too late to see any of the actors before they had left for lunch after their abortive morning.

As Clarence says, I 'passed a dreadful season' waiting for Peggy's return, convinced that my career which had hardly started was already at an end. She arrived back on time, of course, and before I could begin my paragraphs of abject apology, she called the company round her to witness a ceremony. After a brief speech she presented me with a large gift-wrapped box. She had spent the lunchtime organising this 'unwrap the parcel' party joke, and I disposed of layer after layer of wrapping until at long last I came to an old fashioned copper alarm clock with a Union Jack on its face. I looked up to see Peggy bursting with delight and leading a round of applause. Forgiven and made part of the team of which she was the leader, I have been in a state of continual idolatry ever since.

Trevor Nunn

The 1970s

105 *The Plebians Rehearse the Uprising*   1970

Emrys James as the Boss and Peggy Ashcroft as his wife in Gunter Grass's *The Plebians Rehearse the Uprising*, directed by David Jones, for the Royal Shakespeare Company, at the Aldwych Theatre.

A world-famous communist stage director sits on the fence during the East German Uprising of 1953, merely using the revolution as copy for his forthcoming production of *Coriolanus*, thus angering workers and state, who both want his name on their manifestoes.

Gunter Grass denied his play was about Brecht, a disclaimer which deceived nobody, and which was patently absurd when Emrys James was made-up to look like Brecht.

The fact that Peggy Ashcroft was cast as the director's wife, who was playing Volumnia, led most people to expect she would have one good scene at least, but the part was tiny and the scene never materialised.

The most dramatic moment was when it looked as if the workers were going to string Brecht up.

106 *The Lovers of Viorne*   1971

Peggy Ashcroft as Claire Lannes and Gordon Jackson as the interrogator in Marguerite Duras's *The Lovers of Viorne*, directed by Jonathan Hales, for the English Stage Company, at the Royal Court Theatre.

Claire Lannes, having killed her deaf-and-dumb cousin, cut up her body and dropped the pieces, one by one, into passing trains, from the railway bridge of her home-town. She kept only the head.

Peggy Ashcroft's Claire was notable for her extraordinary serenity under interrogation, as if the chilling events being described had nothing to do with her whatsoever.

If this is not great acting, then I do not know what the term means.
Frank Marcus *Sunday Telegraph*

Peggy Ashcroft's Claire is one of the finest schizophrenic performances I have seen.
Irving Wardle *The Times*

There is a wonderful moment when she talks of her lost lover. Her face brims with tears that never fall. But she makes Claire mad. Her mouth works, her fingers endlessly twitch. Her way of life is utter desolation, and it is not surprising that she ended it by murder. In other words Dame Peggy offers an explanation where it is essential there should be no explanation. It is very fine, but it is not Mme Duras' play.
Harold Hobson *Sunday Times*

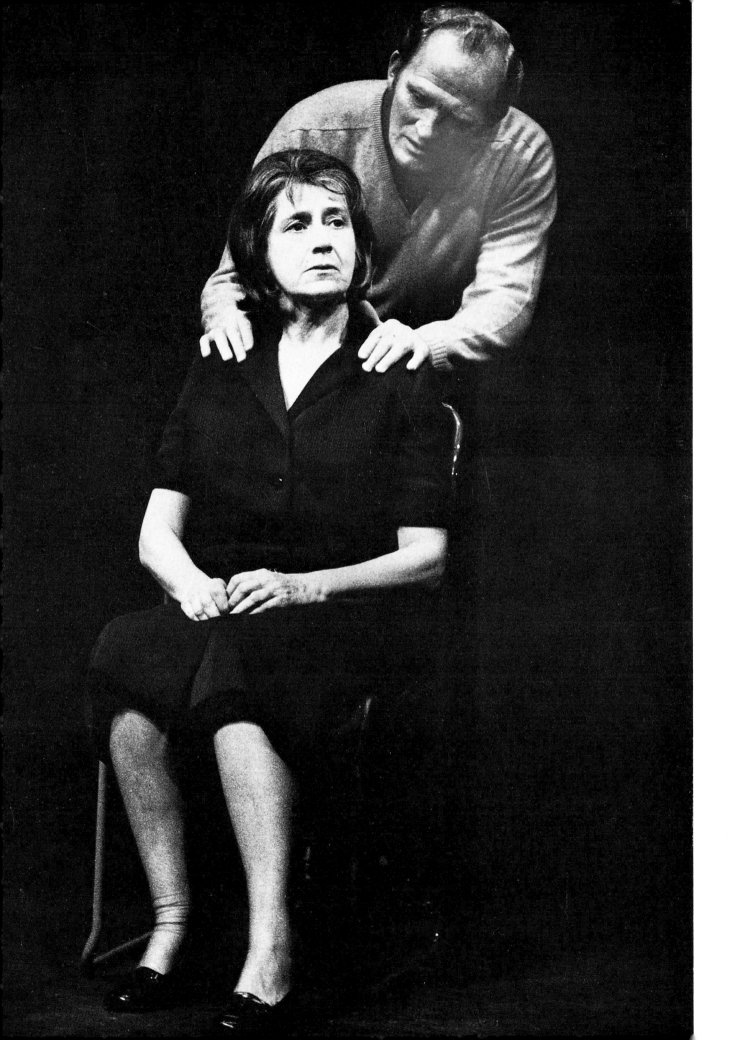

When young actors ask me – and they do frequently, with eyes so eager – 'Who is your favourite actor?' or 'Who is the best actor you've ever worked with?' I find that my mouth, without a thought from my head, guiding, prodding, has formed the words Peggy Ashcroft. We playwrights – although we know better – expect miracles from actors who work in our plays: we expect them to 'become' our characters – lose their own identities, or transfer their souls, if you will, and, at the same time, we expect them to keep the talent, the intellect objective enough to maintain shape, content and meaning. We expect miracles because we are optimists – why else would we write plays? – and because every once in a while we run into someone like Peggy Ashcroft.

Edward Albee

107 *All Over* 1972

Angela Lansbury as the Mistress, Sebastian Shaw as the Best Friend and Peggy Ashcroft as the Wife in Edward Albee's *All Over*, directed by Peter Hall, for the Royal Shakespeare Company, at the Aldwych Theatre.

All Over, elegiac yet savage, was Albee's best play since *Who's Afraid of Virginia Woolf?*

A famous man lies dying in a four-poster. His family, mistress, best friend gather. Who he is we never learn, so busy are they all talking about themselves. Their individual and collective suffering is turned into a series of acrimonious arias. It was like watching and listening to a modern Greek tragedy in a pannelled room.

The technical skill, with which the whole cast, in a fine bit of ensemble playing, handled Albee's highly artificial and tortuous Jamesian syntax, was most impressive. The acting, like the play, had a hard veneer; and the production, an embalmed elegance.

Peggy Ashcroft, as the great man's wife, was all artic wit and malicious cruelty. It was a beautifully taut, incisive performance, until a memorable breakdown into tears, the last line, 'Because . . . I'm . . . unhappy,' being repeated four times, in a mixture of self-loathing and self-pitying.

108 *Lloyd George Knew My Father* 1972

Ralph Richardson as General Sir William Boothroyd and Peggy Ashcroft as Lady Boothroyd in William Douglas Home's *Lloyd George Knew My Father*, directed by Robin Midgley at the Savoy Theatre.

Lady Boothroyd threatens to kill herself if the planning authorities go ahead and build a by-pass through her park.

There was no difficulty whatsoever in believing that Peggy Ashcroft (who, after all, had once canvassed 10 Downing Street, at election time, to vote for the Opposition) *would* make a stand; but the part offered her fewer comic opportunities than it did Sir Ralph, and the play was so trivial that many people wondered what they were doing in it.

109 *The Last Journey* *1972*

Harry Andrews and Peggy Ashcroft as Leo and Sonja Tolstoy in James Forsyth's *The Last Journey*, directed by Peter Potter for Granada Television.

Peggy Ashcroft and Harry Andrews were very moving in this play about the last days of Tolstoy, but the production suffered from having to follow, almost immediately, a television documentary, which had been able to get hold of genuine newsreel pictures of the same event.

I adore Peggy, who has been the most important female influence in my acting career. I first worked with her in Romeo and Juliet in 1935 and appeared with her many times since. By just watching her rehearse and perform, I have learnt, by her shining example, that, though technique and theatrical skills are important, truth is what matters most.

I have many happy memories of Peggy. A typical one is travelling to and from Manchester when we were doing a play about Leo Tolstoy. The television company, as a matter of principle, would only provide second class fares. So Peg, a good socialist, insisted on travelling second, whereas I insisted on paying the extra and travelling in comfort! I well remember the pleasure and amusement it caused her when I went and hob-nobbed with her second class for most of the journey. I reminded her then, how during rehearsals in Brixton, she had been provided with a chauffeur-driven limousine and always offered me a lift to my flat en route to her home in Hampstead – typical of Dame Peggy, God bless her!

Harry Andrews

110 *A Slight Ache* 1973

Richard Pasco as the match-seller and Peggy Ashcroft as Flora in
Harold Pinter's *A Slight Ache*, directed by Peter James, for the
Royal Shakespeare Company, at the Aldwych Theatre.

Flora is a middle-class woman, who exchanges her blustering
and sexually dormant husband for a silent match-seller, a filthy,
balaclavad old tramp.

A Slight Ache, a black comedy, had originally been written for
radio, some ten years earlier, when audiences did not have to see
the symbolic figure and therefore wonder who he was and why he
was being invited into a prosperous suburban home.

Peggy Ashcroft's moving performance was also surprisingly
erotic, and not only when she was voluptuously hugging the
tramp. An ordinary line, like 'When I was a Justice of the Peace,
I had him on the front bench' suddenly took on a whole new
meaning.

A Slight Ache played in tandem with Pinter's *Landscape*.

111 *John Gabriel Borkman* 1975

Peggy Ashcroft as Ella Rintheim, Ralph Richardson as Borkman and Wendy Hiller as Gunhild Borkman in Henrik Ibsen's *John Gabriel Borkman*, directed by Peter Hall, for the National Theatre, at the Old Vic Theatre.

Ella Rintheim is the woman Borkman had loved and sacrificed to his ambition. She has always felt that the son he gave his wife, her twin-sister, is rightfully hers, and, when he is grown-up, she comes to claim him.

Edvard Munch described Ibsen's penultimate play as 'the most powerful winter landscape in Scandinavian art'. Impressive though Peggy Ashcroft was in the long duel with Gunhild for possession of the boy, and in the long climb, realistic and symbolic, of the last act, where she gave Ralph Richardson noble support, there were some critics who did not feel she was wintery enough.

If ever a character were in need of irony it is she. The part is played by Peggy Ashcroft with affectingly honest feeling and matchless lyrical delivery.
Irving Wardle *The Times*

. . . beauty and selflessness, indeed, are everywhere apparent in her performance, sometimes too abtrusively. She emphasises nobility as insistently as Sir Ralph denies it.
Robert Cushman *Observer*

I first worked with Peggy Ashcroft at Stratford in 1957. She was playing Imogen in Cymbeline. It was the first time I had worked with a major, major star and it was a rewarding and provocative experience, which I shall never forget, certainly one of the key things which led me into an understanding of how to work on Shakespeare's texts and indeed how to do Shakespeare. We became friends. In 1958 I worked with her in the West End on a Robert Ardrey play, Shadow of Heroes, about the Hungarian revolution. Then, in the same year, I was asked to take over the Stratford Festival at the then-called Shakespeare Memorial Theatre, and I put forward plans to the Board to form a Company based on contract artists, a continuity of actors, directors and designers, and also to open a London theatre, so that an ensemble of people engaged on trying to make Shakespeare work at Stratford would also be in touch with the present by doing modern plays about modern sensibilities in London. The first actor I asked to join this ensemble was Peggy Ashcroft. I thought that if I could get one of the leaders of the profession to endorse the scheme then others would follow. I well remember the moment I asked her. I had taken her out to dinner and we talked about the theatre and what the theatre needed, and how it was necessary, in order to do good work in the theatre, to develop a company feeling, and (as is the way with these things) I didn't have the nerve to ask her the key question until I was driving her home.

We were going round Trafalgar Square in my little Ford Prefect when I said, 'If I manage to get the Stratford Board to agree to this whole scheme of a company, would you be the first actor to join it?' and without hesitation she said 'Yes'.

Now many people are responsible for the founding of the RSC, certainly Sir Fordham Flower, the visionary chairman, and all who had worked at Stratford before, giving us reserves and resources which enabled the company idea to fly. But I have to say that I could not have done what I did without the support and encouragement of Peggy. And this is really talking about her as a woman rather than as an actress. She has enormous idealism, enormous integrity, enormous intelligence. She is always supportive, whatever the consequences, of great humanitarian causes, whether they are to do with nuclear disarmament, with censorship, with the problems that writers and actors have behind the iron curtain. She has a generosity of spirit and a fighting power in any situation which is quite unrivalled. Her dedication is passionate and it spills over into, of course, her work in the theatre as an actress. Her prime concern when she is working is care for the play – what the play means and what the play should convey to the audience. It is for this reason that she believes so strongly in the value of team work.

However great a star you are you cannot behave in a solo fashion

without suffering. Each night when a group of actors meet together on a stage they are dependent on each other. The smaller part actor can wreck a scene for the leading actor unless there is that trust and openness. Peggy knows this and she knows that out of a group, out of sharing, out of understanding, comes real creative work. And because of her history with Komisarjevsky, with Gielgud, with Michel Saint-Denis, she believes in the director – not as the autocrat, but as the outside eye who can give the right information, the right criticism, the right challenge to the group of actors, keep a critical sense. So it is only at the end of the day, because of her blinding talent, that she is a star. She is not a star in the rehearsal room, and she's certainly not a star in performance – someone who thinks of reputation or of being centre stage or all those generalities of vanity. What she believes in is the character and the play and what it should mean.

As an actress she has an inescapable Englishness. Even when she is playing tragedy it is informed with wit and with humour of an utterly English kind. And it seems to me that the great tradition of English wit and irony extends back through her to Edith Evans and to what we know and believe of Ellen Terry. There is a straight line there. She does not sentimentalise characters. She is quite capable of playing the ugliness of the human personality, and she presents a character with warts and all. She knows a fundamental fact which many actors, and particularly stars, fail to recognise. They think they must be liked by the public by always emphasising the likeable side of the character. Actually the reverse is true. If you have the courage to show the faults and failings and ugliness of the character the audience's understanding and compassion is released in a much stronger way.

She has a great sense of character. When she was creating Queen Margaret in The Wars of the Roses with me at Stratford in the 1960s – a part which extended over the Henry VI plays and Richard III, started as a young girl of eighteen and ended as a mad old woman in her seventies – she insisted, in order to get at the particular foreignness and energy of the character, that a very slight French accent was needed, because the princess originally came from France. These tiny points in the accent – a rolling of the 'r's making them slightly obtrusive – absolutely transformed her spirit and made her stronger and genuinely French and provocative. In the same way when we did Happy Days together, the Beckett play, she found a slightly Anglo-Irish lilt which was absolutely the cadence and voice of Sam Beckett himself.

This brings me to another point – her musicality. She has a magnificent voice, trained and developed over many years, and she has like all great stars a particular idiosyncratic way of making Shakespeare beat rhythmically, keeping the line. At the end of a line when Peggy is speaking Shakespeare she slightly stresses the last couple of words or last word of the line. This defines the end of the line, gives the linear structure and makes it move on with great energy. She is a wonderful Shakespeare speaker, not in terms of academic theory but in terms of passion, of always worrying over the text so that she goes with the beat, goes with the rhythm, makes it regular, makes it happen, makes it run on. Again like all great actors – one thinks of Gielgud as well – she speaks tremendously quickly, tremendously lightly, so that the audience run after her. They are in pursuit, eagerly wanting to know what she is saying. And I indeed remember her and Gielgud in Much Ado About Nothing as an extraordinary display of quick-tongued wit, unbelievably fast.

Allied to this wit and this humour there is the fact that in a way, she has remained a young girl. Now we celebrate her as a grand lady of the British theatre about to be eighty. Yet she has the soul of a girl, the naïveté of a girl, the passion of a girl, the wonder of a girl, and that has always informed all her acting. Though the converse is there. She can be dangerous, she can be predatory. I remember how dangerous she was as Hedda Gabler, and yet I remember the pathos and the heartbreak of The Deep Blue Sea. Coming back to Queen Margaret in The Wars of the Roses, that young girl of eighteen was partly the passionate young princess, yet also partly the mad warrior queen carrying a severed head across the battlefield, and partly the mad old lady at the end of Richard III.

She is a complete and extraordinary actress with a great range. She has probably embodied the Shakespeare heroine (Viola, Cleopatra, Ophelia, Desdemona, Beatrice, Rosalind, Juliet, Imogen) with more wit, more femininity, more energy, more naïveté, than any other actress of her time. Her position as a great actor is unquestioned. What I think needs emphasising is her position as a great human being who has spent her life not in making money, not in being a star, but in endorsing the Royal Court with George Devine, the Royal Shakespeare Company with me, and earlier Gielgud's company, Saint-Denis's company, so that the theatre could remain at the centre of our life. She has always been eager to go with the new dramatists and with the new talent, whilst safeguarding the tradition of the British heritage. It was also she who first did Brecht at the Royal Court in The Good Woman of Setzuan. The whole of the British theatre would be poorer and certainly very different were it not for the contribution she has made as a leader.

Peter Hall

112 *Happy Days* 1975

Peggy Ashcroft as Winnie in Samuel Beckett's *Happy Days*, directed by Peter Hall, for the National Theatre, at the Old Vic. The production transferred to the Lyttleton Theatre in 1977.

Winnie, buried first up to her waist and then up to her chin in a mound of earth, prattling away ('There is so little one can say, one says it all and there is no truth in it anywhere') refusing to give way to despair, pain and loneliness, is an Everest of a part, making enormous demands on actress and audience alike.

Peggy Ashcroft, with her rouged cheeks and her silly hat, might momentarily have been mistaken for a suburban housewife having a jolly day at the seaside; but a performance begun in comedy ended in ashen panic-stricken terror, as Winnie scanned the horizon and saw only approaching death.

There was an extraordinary moment, at the end of the play, when it seemed as if husband Willie was actually going to shoot her; certainly the audience, at the Old Vic, presumed that he was crawling up the mound to get the revolver rather than reaching out to touch her. It was one of the biggest laughs of the evening.

It is a memorable performance of someone desperately failing to deceive herself.

Benedict Nightingale *New Statesman*

Peggy Ashcroft is as near perfection as we are likely to see in our time.
B. A. Young *Financial Times*

113 *Old World   1976*

Anthony Quayle as Rodion Nikolayevich and Peggy Ashcroft as
Lidya Vasilyevna in Aleksei Arbuzov's *Old World*, directed by
Terry Hands, for the Royal Shakespeare Company, at the
Aldwych Theatre. The production transferred to the Royal
Shakespeare Theatre, Stratford-upon-Avon.

Old World, a huge success in the Soviet Union, playing in fifty
theatres, was a Baltic *Brief Encounter* between a director of a
sanitorium and one of his more eccentric and rebellious patients,
a box office cashier in the circus where she had once performed.

This episodic, banal and cheaply sentimental two-hander did
not repeat its success in London, where it was generally thought
the actors were wasting their time.

The chief pleasure was watching Peggy Ashcroft and Anthony
Quayle drunkenly charlestoning.

Actors, actresses, live on the balance of a hair between self-confidence (without which they could not walk onto a stage) and self-doubt (without which they would be merely odious). Peggy is a vivid example of this delicate balance.

Confidence leads her into championing every sort of cause: the reincarnation of Joan of Arc. Doubt gives her the vulnerability, that invests even her most positive performances.

At Stratford in 1950 she was about to open as Beatrice in Much Ado About Nothing in a famous production of John Gielgud's. She was uneasy in rehearsals and, on the opening day, burst into sobs in the middle of lunch.

'Peg . . . Darling Peg . . . What ever is the matter?' I asked.

There were more sobs; tears fell into the soup. At last she said:

'It's awful . . . They're going to find out that I'm such a fraud.'

I can think of several actors who perhaps ought to have said those words but it was Peg, the dearest, the least fraudulent actress I have ever known, who actually did say them.

Anthony Quayle

114 *Edward and Mrs Simpson* 1978

Peggy Ashcroft as Queen Mary in *Edward and Mrs Simpson*, directed by Waris Hussein for Thames Television.

The shame and humiliation of the abdication crisis was keenly felt and Peggy Ashcroft made much of the Queen's scene with her son: 'What's love compared to duty? . . . I cannot bear to hear you talk only of your happiness.'

Edward Fox played the wilful king and Cynthia Harris played his American friend.

As Queen Mary, Dame Peggy Ashcroft is quietly giving everyone else on television a lesson in how to act for the camera. Since she so rarely acts for the camera, the secret of her astonishing success must lie not in a specialised training, but on a general ability to accept, employ and transcend any set of technical limitations imposed on her. Dame Peggy is a bit of all right.

Clive James *Observer*

115 *Hullabaloo over George and Bonnie's Pictures* 1978

Peggy Ashcroft as Lady Gee in Ruth Prawer Jhabvala's *Hullabaloo Over George and Bonnie's Pictures*, a film directed by James Ivory.

Hullabaloo Over George and Bonnie's Pictures, originally shown over two *South Bank Shows*, is a gently ironic comedy in the Henry James manner: an Anglo-Indian *The Spoils of Poynton*.

Two rival art collectors vie for a priceless collection of exquisite Indian miniatures. The film raises the question whether the miniatures should stay where they belong and where they are neither seen nor appreciated, gathering dust, or whether they should be brought to America or England.

Peggy Ashcroft gave an amusing portrait of the British Raj in unethical action: she played a very determined curator, who sees it as her *duty* to take the collection back to England. She was particularly funny, when talking to her American rival, while casually throwing luggage onto the roof of her landrover.

116 Mrs Moore in A *Passage to India* 1984 ▷

117 *Watch on the Rhine* 1980

Peggy Ashcroft as Fanny Farrelly in Lilian Hellman's *Watch on the Rhine*, directed by Mike Ockrent at the National Theatre.

Watch on the Rhine, Lilian Hellman's anti-fascist piece, was written in 1940, with the express intention of making American isolationists feel guilty, and getting them involved in the war in Europe; inevitably, forty years after Pearl Harbour, the political propaganda no longer had the urgency to blind an audience to the play's glib drawing-room comedy and old-fashioned melodramatics.

Peggy Ashcroft played a selfish and snobbish matriarch, a rich liberal, living in a handsome colonial house, who has to be shocked out of her ignorance and insularity. Her performance was a perfect marriage of good manners and abrasive rudeness.

118 *Caught on a Train* 1980

Peggy Ashcroft as Frau Messner in Stephen Poliakoff's *Caught on a Train*, directed by Peter Duffell for BBC Television.

Caught on a Train, one of the major television films of the 1980s, which owed something to Kafka and Hitchcock, was essentially a confrontation between two generations: an old lady and a young publisher, mittel European *ancien regime* versus pushy modern Oxbridge, both equally intolerant.

Frau Messner, sharp, abrupt and unmistakably Viennese in her manner, is wonderfully rude, selfish and arrogant. Accustomed to getting her own way, patronising and provocative, her behaviour becomes more and more outrageous. There was a splendid moment, in the restaurant car when, finding she is ignored by the steward, she deliberately drops crockery in the aisle. Frau Messner may well be a member of a dying breed, but there is never any doubt, in any battle for survival, that she will last far longer than the young man ever will.

The great strength of Stephen Poliakoff's script and Peggy Ashcroft's acting was the way our sympathies shifted imperceptibly away from the publisher to her. 'You're good-looking. You're quite clever. You notice things. And you're not at all cruel. But you don't care. You pretend to, of course, you pretend. But you don't really care about anything, do you?'

Frau Messner was one of Peggy Ashcroft's finest performances.

119 Cream In My Coffee 1980

Peggy Ashcroft and Lionel Jeffries as Jean and Bernard Wilsher in Dennis Potter's *Cream In My Coffee*, directed by Gavin Millar for London Weekend Television.

Peggy Ashcroft and Lionel Jeffries were cast as an elderly couple returning, in 1980, to the Grand Hotel, Eastbourne, where they spent a weekend together, in 1934, before they were married.

The construction of the play allowed for the action to be constantly slipping back and forth from the present to the past. The only trouble with this conceit was that it was quite impossible to reconcile Lionel Jeffries's unpleasant old man with his younger persona as played by Peter Chilson.

Peggy Ashcroft, in the more sympathetic role of the unhappy wife, and with far less to say, acting in a quieter and more wistful key, effortlessly conveyed the sorrow and emptiness of her life.

When *Cream In My Coffee* won the 1982 Prix Italia television drama prize, some members of the jury complained that Dennis Potter's bitter-humorous play was 'almost too professional', as if they felt they had been conned into giving the award by the glamorous setting, the author's trick with time and the acting.

120 Recital 1981

Julian Bream and Peggy Ashcroft in *Four centuries of poetry and musical reflections from Shakespeare to Neruda and Bach to Villa Lobos*. The programme was seen in a number of venues, including the Greenwich Theatre, for the Greenwich Festival.

121 All's Well That Ends Well   1981

Harriet Walter as Helena and Peggy Ashcroft as the Countess of
Rousillon in Shakespeare's *All's Well That Ends Well*, directed by
Trevor Nunn, for the Royal Shakespeare Company, at the Royal
Shakespeare Theatre, Stratford-upon-Avon. The production
transferred to the Barbican Theatre in 1982.

Trevor Nunn's production, as brilliant as anything he had ever
done, and far better than the play, was visually stunning, John
Gunter's huge, adaptable glasshouse providing an extremely
handsome First World War setting.

The Countess is the most benevolent character in this cynical
and unpleasant comedy. Peggy Ashcroft acted her with great
charm and compassion: a lovely performance, almost
Chekhovian in its melancholy beauty; though it did seem
somewhat unlikely that the Countess, in this particular period,
would tolerate, let alone listen to, the crudities of the clown,
Lavache, now cast as an Edwardian gamekeeper.

122 *Little Eyolf* *1982*

Peggy Ashcroft as the Rat-Wife in Henrik Ibsen's *Little Eyolf*, directed by Michael Darlow for BBC Television.

This rarely performed play, a study of guilt and remorse in the classical idiom, was given a stylised production and looked stagey enough to transfer as it was, into the West End. Diana Rigg and Anthony Hopkins played the parents of the crippled Eyolf, a metaphor for their burnt-out marriage.

The Rat-Wife, 'searching out things that nibble and gnaw' is a sinister and symbolic role. Peggy Ashcroft was a very aristocratic Pied Piper of the Norwegian fjords.

123 *The Jewel in the Crown* 1984

Yazdani Raz Khan as Ashok and Peggy Ashcroft as Barbie
Batchelor in Paul Scott's *The Jewel in the Crown*, directed by
Christopher Morahan for Granada Television.

The Jewel in the Crown, based on Paul Scott's *Raj Quartet*,
traced the final years of British rule in India, when the two
nations were 'still locked in an imperial embrace of such long-
standing and subtlety, it was no longer possible for them to know
whether they hated or loved one another'.

In an exceptionally strong cast, Peggy Ashcroft, as Barbie
Batchelor, the retired English missionary schoolteacher,
snubbed, patronised and ignored by so many of the Raj
community, came to dominate the series.

Her deeply compassionate performance (never more so than
when she was, so pitifully, looking for her gift of apostle
teaspoons at the wedding) would seem to have moved a whole
nation to tears. There was, too, that moment when the awful
Mildred, permanently drunk, accused her of having 'the soul of a
parlour-maid'. It was Peggy Ashcroft's keen appreciation of
Barbie's pluck, as well as her vulnerability, which was so
beautifully judged.

The Jewel in the Crown, brilliantly sustained over a thirteen-
week period, was compulsive viewing; except, of course, for
those viewers, who, shocked as Barbie was, by what Mildred and
the adjutant were doing under the mosquito net (a key episode in
her mental and spiritual breakdown), turned off their television
sets and wrote to tell the newspapers they had done so.

124 *The Jewel in the Crown* 1984

Peggy Ashcroft as Barbie Batchelor and Fabia Drake as Aunt
Mabel in *The Jewel in the Crown*.

Peggy Ashcroft's performance has been one of the glories of the series.
Lucy Hughes-Hallett   Standard

*Miss Ashcroft's performance is a tour de force which deserves to win
every available award for outstanding acting.*
Richard Ingrams Spectator

Peggy Ashcroft was – but of course – incomparable.
James Cameron Guardian

---

*It was the easiest bit of casting I've ever done. I was on the phone at the
stage door of the National talking to somebody or other about* The
Jewel in the Crown *and I was aware that the actress standing next to
me was whispering at me as I spoke.*

'I want to be in it,' said Dame Peggy. I hung up.

'Certainly,' I said. 'What do you want to play?'

'Barbie Batchelor,' she said.

*That was that (not quite so simple of course – the RSC had to move
heaven and earth and a lot of the schedule at Stratford and the Barbican
to make it possible).*

*She arrived at Simla in a thunderstorm so total that it seemed an
omen. However, it was an omen of good things rather than bad. We
warmed her with blankets, single bar fires, hot water bottles and
protected her with layers of macs while she embarked on a performance
which took her from the heights of the Himalayan foothills to a
warehouse in Manchester, a graveyard in Derbyshire and ended in yet
more rain in a Welsh forest. She was stunning all the time.*

*Afterwards I asked Lord Bernstein about her – about the effect she
must have had on the London theatre world in the thirties.*

'Was she beautiful?' I asked.

'She's beautiful now', he said.

Christopher Morahan

125 A Passage to India 1984

Peggy Ashcroft as Mrs Moore and Victor
Banerjee as Aziz in the film version of
E. M. Forster's *A Passage to India*, directed
by David Lean.

Though Forster had never wanted *A
Passage to India* filmed and would have
been appalled by the new ending, in
which East and West *connect* (Aziz and
Fielding being reconciled), he would,
most certainly, have approved of the
casting of Peggy Ashcroft, having
suggested the role of Mrs Moore to her, as
early as 1962, when the novel was staged
in London.

Mrs Moore's spiritual journey is not the
easiest thing to translate into cinematic
terms, and David Lean's screenplay gave
Peggy Ashcroft very little to get to grips
with. The 'boum' had gone out of the
character.

The old lady's irritation at the Bridge
Party was perfectly caught: the wish, tartly
expressed, that the Collector's ghastly
wife should be retired immediately to
Tunbridge Wells so exactly coincided
with the audience's own feelings that they
applauded.

*When she's on the screen, you cannot take
your eyes off her. Thank God we have at last
got a proper cinematic record of her greatness
as an actress.*
Derek Malcolm *Guardian*

*I predict this remarkable 163-film will be
Peggy Ashcroft's passage to an Oscar.*
Alexander Walker *Standard*

At the Oscar award-winning ceremony,
she was sadly too ill to attend, Peggy
Ashcroft, very characteristically, had
intended to thank India for making
Forster's novel and Lean's film possible.

What can I say that will not seem fulsome? Consummate actress, darling friend, impeccable partner and colleague, a beneficent member of every enterprise and company. She is quite delightfully unchanged and unspoilt by her recent world fame on the screen and television, the same enchanting personality she has always been in the sixty-odd years I have known and cherished her.

John Gielgud

126 *Six Centuries of Verse   1984*

Ralph Richardson, Peggy Ashcroft and John Gielgud in the grounds of Beckley Park, near Oxford, during the filming of the fifth programme of *Six Centuries of Verse*, which was devoted to the work of Shakespeare and directed by Richard Mervyn for Thames Television.

127 *Murder by the Book*   1986

Iam Holm as Hercule Poirot and Peggy Ashcroft as Agatha
Christie in Nick Evans's *Murder by the Book*, directed by
Lawrence Gordon Clark for TVS.

Nick Evans had the amusing idea of Hercule Poirot
investigating his own murder, before it has happened, when he
learns his creator is about to publish a book in which he is to be
bumped off.

Agatha Christie had wanted to get rid of 'the wretched little
man', as early as 1940, but had not been allowed to do so by her
literary agent.

Peggy Ashcroft's reality was a perfect foil for Ian Holm, who
rightly played the Belgian detective as a work of fiction: an absurd
waxwork-caricature irritated by his own absurdity.

128 *A Perfect Spy*   *1987*

Peggy Ashcroft as Miss Dubber in John
Le Carré's *A Perfect Spy*, directed by Peter
Smith for BBC Television

A British spy returns to England for his
father's funeral and disappears, much to
the consternation of two of the world's
intelligence services who are no longer
certain whose side he is on. He chooses as
his retreat a seaside boarding-house run by
Miss Dubber.

129 Peggy Ashcroft 1929 ▷

Chronology

CHRONOLOGY

THEATRE

DATE	PLAY	ROLE	WRITER	DIRECTOR	THEATRE
1926					
May	*Dear Brutus*	Margaret	J. M. Barrie	W. G. Fay	Birmingham Repertory
1927					
May	*One Day More*	Bessie Carvil	Joseph Conrad	Ralph Neale	Playroom Six
May	*The Return*	Mary Dunn	Charles Bennett	Alexander Field	Everyman
Jul	*When Adam Delved*	Eve	George Paston	Nigel Playfair	Q
Sep	*Bird in Hand*	Joan Greenleaf	John Drinkwater	John Drinkwater	Birmingham Repertory
Nov	*The Way of the World*	Betty	William Congreve	Nigel Playfair	Wyndham's
1928					
Jan	*The Fascinating Foundling*	Anastasia Vullimay	Bernard Shaw	Henry Oscar	Arts
Jan	*The Land of Heart's Desire*	Mary Bruin	W. B. Yeats	Henry Oscar	Arts
Jan	*The Silver Cord*	Hester	Sidney Howard	Henry Oscar	Tour
Sep	*Earthbound*	Edith Strange	Leslie Goddard and Cecil Weir	Henry Oscar	Q
Oct	*Easter*	Kristina	August Strindberg translated by Dr E. Classen	Allan Wade	Arts
Nov	*A Hundred Years Old*	Eulalia	Serafin and Joaquin Alvarez Quintero translated by Helen and Harley Granville Barker	A. E. Filmer	Lyric, Hammersmith
1929					
Apr	*Requital*	Lucy Deren	Molly Kerr	Molly Kerr	Everyman
May	*Bees and Honey*	Sally Humphries	H. F. Maltby	H. F. Maltby	Strand
June	*She Stoops to Conquer*	Constance Neville	Oliver Goldsmith	Nigel Playfair	Tour
Sep	*Jew Süss*	Naemi	Ashley Dukes adapted from Lion Feuchtwanger's novel	Matheson Lang and Reginald Denham	Duke of York's
1930					
May	*Othello*	Desdemona	William Shakespeare	Ellen van Volkenburg	Savoy
Sep	*The Breadwinner*	Judy Battle	Somerset Maugham	Athole Stewart	Vaudeville
1931					
Apr	*Hassan*	Pervaneh	James Elroy Flecker	Gibson Cowan	New, Oxford (OUDS)
Apr	*Charles the 3rd*	Angela	Curt Götz adapted by Edgar Wallace	Mrs Edgar Wallace	Wyndham's
Jun	*A Knight Passsed By*	Anne	Jan Fabricus adapted by W. A. Darlington	Jan Fabricus	Ambassadors
Jun	*Sea Fever*	Fanny	Marcel Pagnol adapted by Auriol Lee and John van Druten	Auriol Lee	New
Sep	*Take Two From One*	Marcela	Georgio and Maria Martinez Sierra adapted by Helen and Harley Granville Barker	Theodore Komisarjevksy	Haymarket

DATE	PLAY	ROLE	WRITER	DIRECTOR	THEATRE
1932					
Feb	*Romeo and Juliet*	Juliet	William Shakespeare	John Gielgud	New, Oxford (OUDS)
May	*Le Coçu Magnifique*	Stella	Fernand Crommelynck translated by Ivor Montagu	Theodore Komisarjevsky	Globe
Jun	*The Secret Woman*	Salome Westaway	Eden Phillpots	Nancy Price	Duchess

The Old Vic Company at the Old Vic Theatre and Sadler's Wells Theatre 1932-33

1932					
Sep	*Caesar and Cleopatra*	Cleopatra	Bernard Shaw	Harcourt Williams	
Oct	*Cymbeline*	Imogen	William Shakespeare	Harcourt Williams	
Nov	*As You Like It*	Rosalind	William Shakespeare	Harcourt Williams	

1932					
Nov	*Fräulein Elsa*	Fräulein Elsa	Arthur Schnitzler adapted by Theodore Komisarjevsky	Theodore Komisarjevsky	Kingsway

The Old Vic Company at the Old Vic Theatre and Sadler's Wells Theatre 1932-33

Dec	*The Merchant of Venice*	Portia	William Shakespeare	John Gielgud	
1933					
Jan	*The Winter's Tale*	Perdita	William Shakespeare	Harcourt Williams	
Jan	*She Stoops to Conquer*	Kate Hardcastle	Oliver Goldsmith	Harcourt Williams	
Feb	*Mary Stuart*	Mary Stuart	John Drinkwater	Harcourt Williams	
Mar	*Romeo and Juliet*	Juliet	William Shakespeare	Harcourt Williams	
Mar	*The School for Scandal*	Lady Teazle	Richard Brinsley Sheridan	Harcourt Williams	
Apr	*The Tempest*	Miranda	William Shakespeare	Harcourt Williams	

Sep	*Before Sunset*	Inken Peters	Gerard Hauptman adapted by Miles Malleson	Miles Malleson	Shaftesbury
1934					
Feb	*The Golden Toy*	Vasantesena	Carl Zuckmayer and Dion Titheradge	Ludwig Berger	Coliseum
Oct	*The Life That I Gave Him*	Lucia Maubel	Luigi Pirandello adapted by Clifford Bax	Frank Birch	Little
1935					
Oct	*Mesmer*	Thérèse Paradis	Beverley Nichols	Theodore Komisarjevsky	Tour
Oct	*Romeo and Juliet*	Juliet	William Shakespeare	John Gielgud	New
1936					
May	*The Seagull*	Nina	Anton Chekhov translated by Theodore Komisarjevsky	Theodore Komisarjevsky	New
1937					
Jan	*High Tor*	Lise	Maxwell Anderson	Guthrie McClintic	Martin Beck, New York

John Gielgud's Season at the Queen's Theatre 1937-38

Sep	*Richard II*	Queen	William Shakespeare	John Gielgud	
Nov	*The School for Scandal*	Lady Teazle	Richard Brinsley Sheridan	Tyrone Guthrie	
1938					
Jan	*Three Sisters*	Irina	Anton Chekhov translated by Constance Garnett	Michel Saint-Denis	
Apr	*The Merchant of Venice*	Portia	William Shakespeare	John Gielgud and Glen Byam Shaw	

Oct	*The White Guard*	Yeliena	Michael Bulgakov adapted by Rodney Ackland	Michel Saint-Denis	Phoenix
Dec	*Twelfth Night*	Viola	William Shakespeare	Michel Saint-Denis	Phoenix
1939					
May	*Weep for the Spring*	Isolde	Stephen Haggard	Michel Saint-Denis	Tour
Aug	*The Importance of Being Earnest*	Cecily Cardew	Oscar Wilde	John Gielgud	Globe

DATE	PLAY	ROLE	WRITER	DIRECTOR	THEATRE
1940					
Mar	*Cousin Muriel*	Dinah Sylvester	Clemence Dane	Normal Marshall	Globe
Jun	*The Tempest*	Miranda	William Shakespeare	George Devine and Marius Goring	Old Vic
1941					
Jan	*Rebecca*	Mrs de Winter	Daphne du Maurier	George Devine	Tour
1942					
Oct	*The Importance of Being Earnest*	Cecily Cardew	Oscar Wilde	John Gielgud	Phoenix
1943					
Oct	*The Dark River*	Catherine Lisle	Rodney Ackland	Rodney Ackland	Whitehall

John Gielgud's Season at the Theatre Royal, Haymarket 1944-45

DATE	PLAY	ROLE	WRITER	DIRECTOR	THEATRE
1944					
Oct	*Hamlet*	Ophelia	William Shakespeare	George Rylands	
1945					
Jan	*A Midsummer Night's Dream*	Titania	William Shakespeare	George Rylands	
Apr	*The Duchess of Malfi*	The Duchess	John Webster	Nevill Coghill	
1947					
May	*Edward, My Son*	Evelyn Holt	Robert Morley and Noel Langley	Peter Ashmore	His Majesty's
1948					
Sep	*Edward, My Son*	Evelyn Holt	Robert Morley and Noel Langley	Peter Ashmore	Martin Beck, New York
1949					
Feb	*The Heiress*	Catherine Sloper	Ruth and Augustus Goetz adapted from Henry James's *Washington Square*	John Gielgud	Haymarket

The Shakespeare Memorial Theatre Company in Stratford-upon-Avon 1950

DATE	PLAY	ROLE	WRITER	DIRECTOR	THEATRE
1950					
Jun	*Much Ado About Nothing*	Beatrice	William Shakespeare	John Gielgud	
Jul	*King Lear*	Cordelia	William Shakespeare	John Gielgud	

The Old Vic Company at the Old Vic Theatre 1950-51

DATE	PLAY	ROLE	WRITER	DIRECTOR	THEATRE
Nov	*Twelfth Night*	Viola	William Shakespeare	Hugh Hunt	
1951					
Mar	*Electra*	Electra	Sophocles translated by J. T. Sheppard	Michel Saint-Denis	
May	*The Merry Wives of Windsor*	Mistress Page	William Shakespeare	Hugh Hunt	
1952					
Mar	*The Deep Blue Sea*	Hester Collyer	Terence Rattigan	Frith Banbury	Duchess

The Shakespeare Memorial Theatre Company in Stratford-upon-Avon 1953

DATE	PLAY	ROLE	WRITER	DIRECTOR	THEATRE
1953					
Mar	*The Merchant of Venice*	Portia	William Shakespeare	Denis Carey	
Apr	*Antony and Cleopatra*	Cleopatra	William Shakespeare	Glen Byam Shaw	

The Shakespeare Memorial Theatre Company in London and Europe 1953-54

DATE	PLAY	ROLE	WRITER	DIRECTOR	THEATRE
Nov	*Antony and Cleopatra*	Cleopatra	William Shakespeare	Glen Byam Shaw	Prince's

The tour included: The Hague, Amsterdam, Antwerp, Brussels and Paris

DATE	PLAY	ROLE	WRITER	DIRECTOR	THEATRE
1954					
Sep	*Hedda Gabler*	Hedda Gabler	Henrik Ibsen adapted by Max Faber	Peter Ashmore	Lyric, Hammersmith
Dec	*Hedda Gabler*	Hedda Gabler	Henrik Ibsen adapted by Max Faber	Peter Ashmore	Westminster

Hedda Gabler toured Europe in 1955 and was seen in The Hague, Bremen, Hamburg, Copenhagen and Oslo

DATE	PLAY	ROLE	WRITER	DIRECTOR	THEATRE

The Shakespeare Memorial Theatre Company in Europe and London 1955

1955					
Jun	*King Lear*	Cordelia	William Shakespeare	George Devine	Europe only
Jul	*Much Ado About Nothing*	Beatrice	William Shakespeare	John Gielgud	Europe and Palace, London

The tour included: Vienna, Zurich, The Hague, Amsterdam, Rotterdam, Berlin, Copenhagen, Hanover, Oslo, Bremen and Hamburg

1956					
Apr	*The Chalk Garden*	Miss Madrigal	Enid Bagnold	John Gielgud	Haymarket
Oct	*The Good Woman of Setzuan*	Shen Te	Bertolt Brecht translated by Eric Bentley	George Devine	Royal Court

The Shakespeare Memorial Theatre Company in Stratford-upon-Avon 1957

1957					
Apr	*As You Like It*	Rosalind	William Shakespeare	Glen Byam Shaw	
Jul	*Cymbeline*	Imogen	William Shakespeare	Peter Hall	

1958					
Sep	*Portraits of Women*		devised by Peggy Ashcroft and Ossian Ellis		Lyceum, Edinburgh
Oct	*Shadow of Heroes*	Julia Rajk	Robert Ardrey	Peter Hall	Piccadilly
1959					
Jan	*The Coast of Coromandel*	Eva Delaware	J. M. Sadler	John Fernald	Tour
Nov	*Rosmersholm*	Rebecca West	Henrik Ibsen translated by Ann Jellicoe	George Devine	Royal Court
1960					
Jan	*Rosmersholm*	Rebecca West	Henrik Ibsen translated by Ann Jellicoe	George Devine	Comedy

The Shakespeare Memorial Theatre Company in Stratford-upon-Avon and London 1960-61

1960					
Jun	*The Taming of the Shrew*	Katharina	William Shakespeare	John Barton	Memorial
Aug	*The Winter's Tale*	Paulina	William Shakespeare	Peter Wood	Memorial
Dec	*The Duchess of Malfi*	The Duchess	John Webster	Donald McWhinnie	Aldwych
1961					
Jun	*The Hollow Crown*		devised by John Barton	John Barton	Aldwych

1961					
Jun	*Some Words on Women and Some Women's Words**		devised by Peggy Ashcroft		Senate House, University of London

The Royal Shakespeare Company in Stratford-upon-Avon and London 1961

Oct	*Othello*	Emilia	William Shakespeare	Franco Zeffirelli	Royal Shakespeare†
Dec	*The Cherry Orchard*	Mme Ranesvky	Anton Chekhov version by John Gielgud	Michel Saint-Denis	Royal Shakespeare and Aldwych

1962					
May	*The Vagaries of Love*		devised by John Barton	John Barton	Belgrade, Coventry

The Royal Shakespeare Company in Europe, Stratford-upon-Avon and London 1962-64

Jun	*The Hollow Crown*		devised by John Barton	John Barton	Europe

The tour included: Zurich, Geneva, Amsterdam, Utrecht, The Hague, Rotterdam, Tilburg, Arnheim and Paris

1963					
Jul	*The Wars of the Roses*	Margaret	William Shakespeare	Peter Hall	Royal Shakespeare
1964					
Jan	*The Wars of the Roses*	Margaret	William Shakespeare	Peter Hall	Aldwych

The Wars of the Roses was an adaptation of the three parts of *Henry VI* and *Richard III*, produced as a trilogy: *Henry VI*, *Edward IV* and *Richard III*.
The adaptation was by John Barton

Theatre

DATE	PLAY	ROLE	WRITER	DIRECTOR	THEATRE
1964					
Mar	*The Seagull*	Mme Arkadina	Anton Chekhov translated by Ann Jellicoe	George Devine	Queen's

The Royal Shakespeare Company in Stratford-upon-Avon and London 1964-70

DATE	PLAY	ROLE	WRITER	DIRECTOR	THEATRE
Jul	*The Wars of the Roses*	Margaret	William Shakespeare	Peter Hall	Royal Skakespeare
1966					
Jun	*Days in the Trees*	Mother	Marguerite Duras translated by Sonia Orwell	John Schlesinger	Aldwych
1967					
Jun	*Ghosts*	Mrs Alving	Henrik Ibsen adapted by Denis Cannan from William Archer's translation	Alan Bridges	Aldwych
1969					
Jan	*A Delicate Balance*	Agnes	Edward Albee	Peter Hall	Aldwych
Jul	*Landscape*	Beth	Harold Pinter	Peter Hall	Aldwych
Oct	*Henry VIII*	Queen Katharine	William Shakespeare	Trevor Nunn	Royal Shakespeare
Dec	*Henry VIII*	Queen Katharine	William Shakespeare	Trevor Nunn	Aldwych
1970					
Jul	*The Plebians Rehearse The Uprising*	Volumnia	Gunter Grass translated by Ralph Manheim	David Jones	Aldwych
1971					
Jul	*The Lovers of Viorne*	Claire Lannes	Marguerite Duras translated by Barbara Bray	Jonathan Hales	Royal Court
1972					
Jan	*All Over*	The Wife	Edward Albee	Peter Hall	Aldwych (RSC)
Jul	*Lloyd George Knew My Father*	Lady Boothroyd	William Douglas-Home	Robin Midgley	Savoy

The Royal Shakespeare Company in Europe, London and Canada 1973-74

DATE	PLAY	ROLE	WRITER	DIRECTOR	THEATRE
1973					
May	*Landscape*	Beth	Harold Pinter	Peter Hall	Europe
May	*A Slight Ache*	Flora	Harold Pinter	Peter James	Europe
The tour included: Antwerp, Wiesbaden, Essen, Bonn, Bad-Godesburg, Amsterdam, Rotterdam and The Hague					
Oct	*Landscape*	Beth	Harold Pinter	Peter Hall	Aldwych
Oct	*A Slight Ache*	Flora	Harold Pinter	Peter James	Aldwych
1974					
Mar	*The Hollow Crown*			devised by John Barton	Ottawa

The National Theatre at the Old Vic 1975

DATE	PLAY	ROLE	WRITER	DIRECTOR	THEATRE
May	*Tribute to the Lady*	Lilian Baylis	devised by Val May	Val May	Old Vic
1975					
Jan	*John Gabriel Borkman*	Ella Rentheim	Henrik Ibsen translated by Inga-Stina Ewbank and Peter Hall	Peter Hall	Old Vic
Mar	*Happy Days*	Winnie	Samuel Beckett	Peter Hall	Old Vic
Oct	*Dear Liar*	Mrs Patrick Campbell	correspondence of Bernard Shaw and Mrs Patrick Campbell adapted by Jerome Kilty	Edwin Stephenson	Citadel, Edmonton, Canada
1976					
Feb	*Tribute to the Lady*	Lilian Baylis	devised by Val May	Val May	Old Vic (NT)

The Royal Shakespeare Company in London and Stratford-upon-Avon 1976-77

DATE	PLAY	ROLE	WRITER	DIRECTOR	THEATRE
Oct	*Old World*	Lidya Vasilyevna	Aleksei Arbuzov translated by Ariadne Nikolaeff	Terry Hands	Aldwych
1977					
Mar	*Old World*	Lidya Vasilyevna	Aleksei Arbuzov translated by Ariadne Nikolaeff	Terry Hands	Royal Shakespeare

154

DATE	PLAY	ROLE	WRITER	DIRECTOR	THEATRE
The National Theatre 1980-81					
Sep	*Happy Days*	Winnie	Samuel Beckett	Peter Hall	Lyttleton
Sep	*Happy Days*	Winnie	Samuel Beckett	Peter Hall	Citadel, Edmonton, Canada
1980					
Sep	*Watch on the Rhine*	Fanny Farelly	Lilian Hellman	Mike Ockrent	Lyttleton
1981					
Feb	*Family Voices*	Voice 2	Harold Pinter	Harold Pinter	Platform
The Royal Shakespeare Company in Stratford-upon-Avon and London 1981-82					
Nov	*All's Well That Ends Well*	Countess of Rousillon	William Shakespeare	Trevor Nunn	Royal Shakespeare
1982					
Jul	*All's Well That Ends Well*	Countess of Rousillon	William Shakespeare	Trevor Nunn	Barbican
1986					
Feb	*Save the Wells*	Lilian Baylis	devised by Val May	Keith Gray and Richard Gregson	Royal Opera House
Jun	*The Hollow Crown*		devised by John Barton		Swan

* *Some Words on Women and Some Women's Words* was seen in Zurich and Basle in 1962, Israel and Greece in 1965 and Bergen and Oslo in 1978
† The Shakespeare Memorial Theatre was renamed the Royal Shakespeare Theatre in 1961.

FILM

RELEASE DATE	FILM	ROLE	SCREENPLAY	DIRECTOR
1933	*The Wandering Jew*	Ollalla Qintana	H. Fowler Mear from play by E. Temple Thurston	Maurice Elvey
1935	*The Thirty-Nine Steps*	Mrs Crofter	Charles Bennett and Alma Reville from novel by John Buchan	Alfred Hitchcock
1936	*Rhodes of Africa* (US title: *Rhodes*)	Anna Carpenter	Michael Barringer, Leslie Arliss, Miles Malleson from book by Sarah Millin	Berthold Viertel
1940	*Channel Incident*	The Woman	Dallas Bower	Anthony Asquith
1941	*Quiet Wedding*	Fleur Lisle	Terence Rattigan, Anatole de Grunwald based on play by Esther McCracken	Anthony Asquith
1942	*New Lot*	ATS Girl		Carol Reed
1958	*The Nun's Story*	Mother Mathilde	Robert Anderson based on book by Kathryn C. Hulme	Fred Zinnemann
1968	*Secret Ceremony*	Aunt Hanna	George Tabori based on short story by Marco Denevi	Joseph Losey
1969	*Three Into Two Won't Go*	Belle	Edna O'Brien based on novel by Andrea Newman	Peter Hall
1971	*Sunday, Bloody Sunday*	Mrs Greville	Penelope Gilliatt	John Schlesinger
1975	*Der Fussgänger* (English title: *The Pedestrian*)	Lady Gray	Maximillian Schell	Maximillian Schell
1976	*Joseph Andrews*	Lady Tattle	Allan Scott, Chris Bryant based on screenstory by Tony Richardson and novel by Henry Fielding	Tony Richardson
1978	*Hullabaloo Over George and Bonnie's Pictures*	Lady Gee	Ruth Prawer Jhabvala	James Ivory
1984	*A Passage to India*	Mrs Moore	David Lean based on novel by E. M. Forster and play by Santha Rami Rau	David Lean
1987	*When The Wind Blows*	Hilda (voice only)	Raymond Briggs	Jimmy T. Murakami

* *The Wandering Jew* was re-edited and re-released in 1939 as *A People Eternal*

TELEVISION

DATE	TITLE	ROLE	WRITER	DIRECTOR	COMPANY
1939	*The Tempest*	Miranda	William Shakespeare	Dallas Bower	BBC
	Twelfth Night	Viola	William Shakespeare	Michel Saint-Denis	BBC
1958	*Shadow of Heroes*	Julia Rajk	Robert Ardrey	Peter Hall	BBC
1961	*The Class*	Voice only		John Schlesinger	BBC
1962	*The Cherry Orchard*	Mme Ranesvky	Anton Chekhov a version by John Gielgud	Michel Saint-Denis	BBC
1964	*The Wars of the Roses*	Margaret	William Shakespeare adapted by John Barton	Peter Hall	BBC
1965	*Rosmersholm*	Rebecca West	Henrik Ibsen translated by Michael Meyer	Michael Barry	BBC
1966	*Days in the Trees*	Mother	Marguerite Duras translated by Sonia Orwell	Waris Hussein	BBC
	Dear Liar	Mrs Patrick Campbell	correspondence of Bernard Shaw and Mrs Patrick Campbell adapted by Jerome Kilty	Christopher McMaster	Granada
1968	*From Chekhov With Love*	Olga Knipper	translated by Moura Budberg and Gordon Latta adapted by Jonathan Miller	Bill Turner	Rediffusion
1971	*The Last Journey*	Sonia Tolstoy	James Forsyth	Peter Potter	Granada
1978	*Edward and Mrs Simpson*	Queen Mary	Simon Raven based on *Edward VIII* by Lady Francis Donaldson	Waris Hussein	Thames
1980	*Caught on a Train*	Frau Messner	Stephen Poliakoff	Peter Duffell	BBC
	Cream in My Coffee	Jean Wilsher	Dennis Potter	Gavin Millar	London Weekend
1982	*Little Eyolf*	The Rat-Wife	Henrik Ibsen translated by Michael Meyer	Michael Darlow	BBC
1984	*The Jewel in the Crown*	Barbie Batchelor	Paul Scott's *Raj Quartet* adapted by Ken Taylor	Christopher Morahan	Thames
	Six Centuries of Verse		William Shakespeare	Richard Mervyn	Thames
1986	*Murder by the Book*	Agatha Christie	Nick Evans	Lawrence Gordon Clark	TVS
1987	*A Perfect Spy*	Miss Dubber	John Le Carré adapted by Arthur Hopcraft	Peter Smith	BBC

RADIO

1930	*Danger*		*Alexander Nevsky*		*The Blessed Damosel*
1931	*Hamlet*		*Mary Rose*	1945	*A Midsummer Night's Dream*
1932	*Othello*	1942	*Distant Point*	1946	*The Barretts of Wimpole Street*
	A Hundred Years Old		*Quality Street*		*Comus*
1933	*Twelfth Night*		*The Rape of the Lock*		*Island Anthology*
1934	*Measure for Measure*		*Twelfth Night*		*She Married Again*
	Cymbeline		*Alexander Nevsky*		*A Time for Verse*
1935	*Berkeley Square*		*Homage to a King*		*New Poems*
	The Lover		*Dnieper Dam*	1947	*Twelfth Night*
	The Breadwinner		*The Seagull*		*Romeo and Juliet*
1939	*Cyrano de Bergerac*	1943	*The Spirit of France*	1948	*The Bronze Horse*
	Arms and the Man		*The Battle of the Marne*		*The Rape of Lucrece*
1940	*I Was Hitler's Prisoner*		*Mendelssohn Biography*		*A programme on Emily Bronte*
	This is Illyria, Lady		*Butterfly on the Wheel*	1949	*Return to the Old Vic*
	The Barretts of Wimpole Street		*Epithalamium*	1951	*The Pleasure Is Mine*
	The Importance of Being Earnest	1944	*Distant Point*		*Time for Verse*
1941	*A Month in the Country*		*The Hostage*	1953	*Romeo and Juliet*

156

	The Merchant of Venice	1968	*Side*		*Dearest Hope*
	Antony and Cleopatra		*Landscape*		*In the Unlikely Event of an Emergency*
1954	*By Heart*	1970	*The Lady of Shallott*		*The Day War Broke Out* (interview)
	The Duchess of Malfi		*Interview on Leonard Woolf*	1980	*Marie Corell – the Swan of Stratford*
	A Lover's Complaint	1971	*The Father*		*Ouida*
1955	*Two Sonnets by Shakespeare*		*Hay Fever*		*A Generation of Giants* (three interviews)
	Interview on Hedda Gabler		*Remembering Michel Saint-Denis*	1981	*Family Voices*
1957	*Desert Island Discs*	1972	*Emperor of the Sea*		*Chances*
	The Good Woman of Setzuan		*Days in the Trees*		*Yesterday's News*
	Hedda Gabler	1973	*The Life and Times of Queen Victoria*		*A Lady's Life in the Rockie Mountains*
	Cymbeline	1974	*Lady Caroline Lamb*		*Kaleidoscope* (interview)
	As You Like It	1976	*Tribute to the Lady (Lilian Baylis)*	1982	*Desert Island Discs*
1958	*The Ring and the Book Part V*		*The Waves*		*Memoir of Kenneth More*
	Interview on Woman's Hour		*Interview on Edith Evans*		*Talk on Harold Pinter's Plays*
1959	*Poems by Rabindranath Tagore*	1977	*Vivat Rex*	1984	*You Can't Shut Out The Human Voice*
1960	*Poems by J. Scovell*		*Peggy Ashcroft on the Stage*	1985	*Sense and Nonsense*
	Interview on Chekhov's Anniversary		*Theatre Call*		*Days in the Trees*
1961	*The Hollow Crown*	1978	*A Bit of Singing and Dancing*		*Woman's Hour Guest of the Week*
1966	*Macbeth*		*Prefaces to Shakespeare: Romeo and Juliet*	1986	*The Blue Jug*
	Portrait of George Devine		*Moments of Being*		*Interview on Laurence Olivier*
	Poetry Recital from Westminster Abbey	1979	*Beckett at the National*		
1967	*Madam Liberality*		*The Girl Who Came to Supper*		All productions for the BBC

RECORDINGS

WRITER	TITLE	COMPANY
Major recordings include:		
Lord Byron	*Don Juan Cantos I and II*	Argo
Geoffrey Chaucer	*The Wife of Bath*	Caedmon
Katherine Mansfield	*The Garden Party*	Cover to Cover Cassettes
Alexander Pope	*The Rape of the Lock*	Argo
William Shakespeare	*Celebration du quatrieme centenaire de Shakespeare*	UNESCO
	Much Ado About Nothing	Argo
	Othello	Argo
	The Rape of Lucrece	Argo
	Richard III	Caedmon
	The Taming of the Shrew	Argo
	Venus and Adonis	Argo
	The Winter's Tale	Caedmon
	The World of Shakespeare	Argo
Bernard Shaw and Ellen Terry	*The Shaw-Terry Letters*	Caedmon
Edith Sitwell	*Façade*	
Poetry Anthologies	*Elizabethan and Jacobean Lyric*	Argo
	More Favourite Poems	Argo
	Poetry Readings	Decca
	Sense and Nonsense	Argo
	Your Favourite Poems	Argo
	The World of Peggy Ashcroft and John Gielgud	Decca

AWARDS AND HONOURS

1943	Started the Apollo Society
1947	Ellen Terry Award for Evelyn Holt in *Edward, My Son*
1949	The Sketch Award for outstanding achievement in the theatre for Catherine Sloper in *The Heiress*
1951	CBE
1955	King's Gold Medal by Haakon of Norway for Hedda Gabler in *Hedda Gabler*
1956	DBE
	Evening Standard Drama Award for Miss Madrigal in *The Chalk Garden*
	Plays and Players Award for Miss Madrigal in *The Chalk Garden*
1957	Plays and Players Award for Rosalind in *As You Like It*
	Elected to English Stage Company Council
1961	Hon. D. Litt. Oxford University
1962	Ashcroft Theatre, Croydon, opened
	Paris Festival Théâtre des Nations Award for *The Hollow Crown*
1962-64	Member of the Arts Council
1964	Evening Standard Drama Award for Queen Margaret in *The Wars of the Roses*
	Variety Club of Great Britain Award for Queen Margaret in *The Wars of the Roses*
	Hon. D. Litt. Leicester University
	Hon. Fellow of St Hugh's College, Oxford University
1965	Hon. D. Litt. London University
1968	Director of the Royal Shakespeare Company
1969	Plays and Players London Theatre Critics' Award for Agnes in *A Delicate Balance* and Beth in *Landscape*
1971	Plays and Players London Theatre Critics' Award for Claire Lannes in *The Lovers of Viorne* and Queen Katharine in *Henry VIII*
1972	Hon. D. Litt. Cambridge University
1974	Hon. D. Litt. Warwick University
1976	Society of West End Theatre Awards for Lidya Vasilyevna in *Old World*

	Evening Standard Drama Award special award for fifty years in the theatre
	Comdr Order of St Olav
1980	British Academy of Film and Television Arts Award for Frau Messner in *Caught on a Train* and Jean Wilsher in *Cream in My Coffee*
1981	XXème Festival International de Télévision de Monte Carlo for Frau Messner in *Caught on a Train*
	British Press Guild Award for Frau Messner in *Caught on a Train* and Jean Wilsher in *Cream in My Coffee*
1983	British Theatre Association special award to mark her career in the theatre
1984	Royal Television Society Award for Barbie Batchelor in *The Jewel in the Crown*
	Broadcasting Press Guild Television Award for Barbie Batchelor in *The Jewel in the Crown*
	British Academy of Film and Television Arts Award for Barbie Batchelor in *The Jewel in the Crown*
	Academy of Motion Pictures Arts and Sciences Award 'Oscar' for Mrs Moore in *A Passage to India*
	Golden Globe Award for Mrs Moore in *A Passage to India*
	New York Film Critics' Circle Award for Mrs Moore in *A Passage to India*
	Los Angeles Film Critics' Circle for Mrs Moore in *A Passage to India*
	National Board of Review Award for Mrs Moore in *A Passage to India*
1985	British Academy of Film and Television Arts Award for Mrs Moore in *A Passage to India*
	Hollywood South Award for Mrs Moore in *A Passage to India*
	International TV Movies Festival USA Award for Barbie Batchelor in *The Jewel in the Crown*
1986	Hon. D. Litt. Open University
	Hon. D. Litt. Bristol University
	Hon. D. Litt. Reading University

INDEX

Numbers in roman refer to plate captions; numbers in **bold** refer to pages.

ACKNOWLEDGEMENTS

The author would like to begin by expressing his deep appreciation to Dame Peggy Ashcroft for all her help and kindness.

The author would like also to thank the contributors, the photographers, his editor Richard Cohen and his designer Margaret Fraser.

The author and the publisher would like to express their appreciation to the following for their assistance and/or permission to reproduce the photographs. Every effort has been made to trace copyright owners and the author and the publisher would like to apologise to anyone whose copyright has unwittingly been infringed.

Numbers refer to plate captions.

Collection Peggy Ashcroft: 6, 7, 20, 41, 50, 55, 84, 85, 98; BBC Enterprises: 118, 122, 128; BBC Hulton Picture Library: 2, 44, 46; Cecil Beaton, courtesy of Sotheby's, London: 53, 57, 58, 59; Birmingham Repertory Theatre: 8; Cannon Distributors: 5, 116, 125; Zoë Dominic: 97, 101, 103, 107, 110, 111, 112, 113, 117; Granada Television: 109, 123, 124; Guy Gravett: 79, 80; John Haynes: 121; Thomas Holte Theatre Photographic Collection: 93, 94; Merchant Ivory Productions: 115; London Weekend Television: 119; Raymond Mander and Joe Mitchenson Theatre Collection: 6, 9, 12, 14, 15, 16, 17, 18, 21, 22, 23, 24, 25, 26, 27, 28, 29, 31, 32, 36, 60, 61, 62; Angus McBean, Harvard Theatre Collection: 1, 3, 47, 49, 51, 52, 54, 64, 65, 66, 70, 71, 72, 73, 74, 77, 78, 81, 82, 87, 88, 90, 92; Daniel Meadows: 120; National Film Archives: 30, 37, 38, 56, 83, 99, 100, 115; Maurice Newcombe: 91, 96, 102, 104, 105, 106, 108; The Rank Organisation: 37, 38; Houston Rogers, courtesy of Theatre Museum, London: 39, 40, 42, 43, 45, 48, 63; Shakespeare Centre Library, Stratford-upon-Avon: 4, 19, 35; Thames Television: 114, 126; Theatre Musuem, London: 11, 33, 34; Times Newspapers: 10, 13, 86, 95; TVS: 127; John Vickers Archives: 67, 68, 69; Twickenham Film Studios: 30; UIP: 56, 99, 100; Warner Bros: 83.

The author would like to add a personal note of thanks to: Anita Appel, Laurence Bernes, Lydia Cullen, Gillian Edwards-Jones, Sheila Formoy and H.M. Tennent Ltd, Peter Hirst, Jane Judge, Angus McKay, Marjorie Pepe, M. Roffey, Peter Seward, Mary White and everybody at the BFI stills and reference library.